Felix Bittmann
Stata

Felix Bittmann

Stata

───

A Really Short Introduction

DE GRUYTER
OLDENBOURG

ISBN 978-3-11-061729-0
e-ISBN (PDF) 978-3-11-061716-0
e-ISBN (EPUB) 978-3-11-061719-1

Library of Congress Control Number: 2018960701

Bibliographic information published by the Deutsche Nationalbibliothek
The Deutsche Nationalbibliothek lists this publication in the Deutsche Nationalbibliografie;
detailed bibliographic data are available on the Internet at http://dnb.dnb.de.

© 2019 Walter de Gruyter GmbH, Berlin/Boston
Cover image: Felix Bittmann
Typesetting: Integra Software Services Pvt. Ltd.
Printing and binding: CPI books GmbH, Leck

www.degruyter.com

Contents

List of Notes

https://doi.org/10.1515/9783110617160-201

1 Introduction

Congratulations! As you are holding his book in your hands right now, this probably means you want to (or have to) work with Stata, the best statistical software package available! It does not matter whether you are completely new to the field of data sciences or an experienced veteran, Stata will hopefully enable you to answer your research questions correctly, efficiently and in an enjoyable fashion. As you bought this book for a really short and direct introduction, let's skip the formal chit-chat and start right away.

What this book is not

This is not a book about statistics. We will not talk about mathematical techniques, formal hypothesis testing or algorithms for regressions. We will get down to business and start managing and analyzing data. This means you should know about basic statistical concepts, like what a mean is, how to read a table or what a regression is supposed to do.

What this book is

You are now probably sitting in front of a screen, at home or in class, trying to make sense of a collection of data using software you don't know. This book will enable you to manage, assess, manipulate and analyze your data. Your field of study, for example sociology, psychology or political sciences, is of less relevance, as the methods and tools we will see, work with all kinds of datasets. You can use this book for self-study or in addition to your classes (or for self-study after you have skipped all your classes).

Please...

When you like this book, tell your friends and colleagues, as it might help them getting to know Stata. If you don't like this book, tell me, so I have the chance to make things better in the next edition. You can always send emails to mail@statabook.com.

Thank you!

This book has benefited enormously from people who supported me. I want to thank Bill Rising, Dahla Rodewald, Elsje Nieboer, Marie Pauline Burkart, Markus Kreggenwinkel, Minh Nguyet Pham, Steffen Schindler, Svenja Dilger and Viktoria Sophie Zorn. Furthermore I want to acknowledge that the general outline of this book is based on the teachings of Michael Gebel (while I take responsibility for any errors remaining)!

1.1 Formatting

To make reading and finding things easier, this book uses formatting to highlight text. Stata commands are printed like this

https://doi.org/10.1515/9783110617160-001

```
use "testfile.dta"
```

You can enter these commands directly or write them in do-files. Point-and-click pathways are written in **bold**.

Some additional information (Notes), that can be skipped by the reader in a hurry, are printed in boxes separated by horizontal bars. However, you are strongly advised to come back later and have a look.

Some headings are marked with an asterisk (*). These chapters contain slightly more advanced topics that might not be interesting for your very first seminar paper with Stata (but maybe for your second).

Some Stata commands can be abbreviated and are thus easier to type. Within a few hours of use you will also come to the conclusion that the shorter form is often preferable. Throughout the book, we will always use the complete form, yet underline the part that is the alternative short command, for example

```
tabulate age
```

could also be written shorter as

```
tab age
```

Please note that I will not always provide *the* shortest abbreviation possible, but the command that I encountered most often in my work and the work of others.

1.2 Graphic style

This book is printed without colors, therefore, all graphics are in black and white. While this is fine for most outputs Stata generates, some use colors to highlight differences between groups. To visualize these differences without colors, a certain color style (scheme) is used (Bischof, 2017).[1] Therefore, visually, the results presented in this book might differ slightly from what you see on your computer screen (while the interpretation is identical). When you want to receive the exactly same output you have to set the scheme when you start Stata. You can do this by entering the following in your command line

```
ssc install blindschemes, replace      //Download scheme
set scheme plotplain                   //Set scheme as standard
```

---

1 This works for version 12 or newer.

Now Stata will employ this style every time it produces a graphic. To revert to the standard settings either restart Stata or enter

```
set scheme s2color        //Revert to standard settings
```

1.3 Version info

This book is written for Stata 15. If your interface, icons, graphs, tables or path descriptions are slightly off, it may be that you are using a different version. This might be somewhat inconvenient, yet the basic commands are in almost all cases identical.

Throughout the book, we will mostly rely on one dataset, the NLSW88 data. The dataset can always be downloaded using the command

```
webuse nlsw88
```

or you can download it manually from Stata's website[2] for Stata 8 or newer.

1.4 Online resources

You can find complete do-files for every chapter as well as additional material online (www.statabook.com).

1.5 Cheat sheet

Throughout the book, you will learn many commands that you don't need to memorize. However, it can be helpful to write down important information by hand, which will also help you remember it better. Finally, I want to recommend some excellent cheat sheets which were created by Tim Essam and Laura Hughes. Beginners and experts will find these equally useful.[3]

---

2 http://www.stata-press.com/data/r8/nlsw88.dta (2018-02-05).
3 https://geocenter.github.io/StataTraining/ (2018-11-06)

2 The first steps

Let's get started! I will assume that Stata is installed and running on your computer. In this chapter you will learn what Stata looks like, how to open and save files and document your work.

2.1 The graphical user interface (GUI)

You will (hopefully!) see this screen (Figure 2.1)[1]:

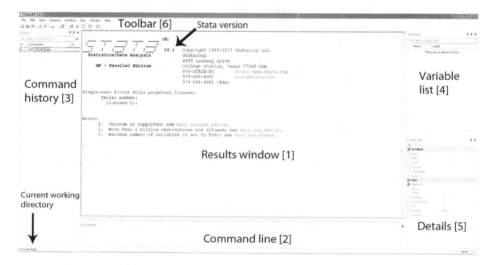

Figure 2.1: The Stata GUI.

Basically, there are six different areas.

1. the largest part, is the **Results window**. Here you will see the commands you entered as well as the corresponding output, that means, the results Stata calculated for you.
2. is the **Command line**, where you enter commands and tell Stata what to do. Most new users who are used to point-and-click are often afraid of commands, as they seem like crazy gibberish only hackers would use. The great thing about

---

1 If what you see is completely different, someone before you might have customized Stata. To return to Factory (Standard) settings, click **Edit → Preferences → Manage Preferences → Factory Settings**. But please make sure to ask your colleagues before if you work on a shared computer!

https://doi.org/10.1515/9783110617160-002

Stata is that you don't have to use the command line as almost all methods can be run with point-and-click as well. Yet with more experience you will naturally come to the conclusion that it is faster and more efficient using some commands. Stata is not about memorizing abstract keywords but about getting stuff done. Throughout the book, I will provide commands and point-and- click pathways for most methods.

3. is the **Command history**, where all commands, either entered by you manually or automatically created by Stata after a point-and-click, will appear. This is of great value as it makes it easy to check what you have already done with your data, and save your work history for replication purposes.

4. shows all variables that are included in your dataset. As you can only have one dataset open at a time in Stata, this list always refers to your currently opened data file. One great feature of this window is the little search bar at the top: you can enter any text and Stata will show any matches within variable names or variable labels, which makes finding the desired variable extremely convenient.

5. will display detailed information about the variable you clicked on in the variable list window. Here you can see the full name, labels (more about that later) or notes. When working with large datasets with many variables, this information can help you a lot when it comes to identifying the correct variable.

6. is the **Toolbar**, where you can click to reach all needed commands and tools.

The arrow at the top shows the current version of Stata which is installed on your computer. Now and then, updates bring cool new features, methods or correct bugs. Luckily, the basics are the same for most versions and will not change anytime soon, meaning that you can read this book using version 10, 15 or any future release of Stata

The arrow at the bottom shows your current working directory, which is explained below.

2.2 Opening stata files

Chances are great that you already have a Stata data file (which you can recognize by the suffix .dta). If this is not the case, we will talk about entering your own data or importing datasets from other software below. You could open the file right away, but you probably have several data files in the same folder. It is a good habit to establish one working folder (with the possibility of sub-folders) to structure your data. Your results and efficiency will definitely benefit from doing this! To change the current working folder, click **File → Change Working Directory** and select the desired folder or enter the following command in the command line (then hit Enter):

```
cd "C:/Users/username/stata-course/"²
```

Please note that the quotation marks are required when your folder name includes spaces. You probably want to see which files are contained in your current working directory. Just type *dir* or *ls*.

Filenames and paths

One of the great things about Stata is that it runs on almost all systems: Windows, Linux and Mac. Virtually all commands and methods will work the same on any computer. Minor differences are due to different file systems and folder structures. For example, a correctly specified path on Windows looks something like:

```
C:\Users\username\stata-course\example.dta
```

while on Linux or Mac, it looks like

```
/home/username/stata-course/example.dta
```

Note the different separators (\VS/). Luckily Stata knows how to deal with this problem and automatically translates separators if needed. Therefore, it is recommended to use the Linux/Mac version like this:

```
cd "C:/Users/username/stata-course/example.dta"
```

This command will work on Windows, Linux and Mac as long as the respective path exist. Throughout the book we will, therefore, use this notation as it is compatible with all systems.

Assuming the file you want to open is in your current working directory, type

```
use "filename.dta"
```

or just

```
use "filename"
```

as the extension is optional and Stata will recognize the correct file. When the file is not in the current working directory, you can use an absolute pathway. For example, type

```
use "C:/Users/username/stata-course/filename.dta"
```

---

2 Of course, you must change my generic example path between the quotation marks to the path where your own files are located on your computer. Also read the next info box to understand why Stata uses different path separators than Windows.

Alternatively use **File → Open** and select the desired file. By the way, this command also works for opening files directly from the Internet:

```
use "http://www.stata-press.com/data/r8/nlsw88.dta"
```

2.3 Importing non-Stata file formats

Sometimes your dataset is not directly available as a Stata .dta file. In this case you can import some other formats, for example from Excel, SAS, XML, Comma Separated Values or unformatted text data. You can see all options by clicking **File → Import**. When you click the desired format, a dialogue will open and help you with importing the data. Other options can be inspected by typing

```
help import
```

Unfortunately there is still no quick option for importing files created from SPSS (.sav) directly into Stata. Luckily there exists a user written command (community-contributed software or CCS). Please refer to page 9, to learn how you can install this little helper program into Stata.

2.4 Entering data manually

Sometimes you want to enter data by hand. This is feasible when there are only tiny bits of information, or for testing purposes. Most datasets from the real world are often very large, containing information about thousands of people (or whatever you study). Entering these amounts of information by hand is clearly insane and not advised as it is time-consuming and very error-prone.

To fill in your data values, enter

```
edit
```

or click the **Data Editor (Edit)** button. A new window will pop up (the Data Editor, Figure 2.2) that displays raw information. Each line (row) stands for one case (observation/person). The variables are shown in the columns on top (grey cells). Double-click one of these and a new window will appear. Enter the name of the variable (for example *age*) and choose "Fill with missing data". Click OK.

Now you can click the cells below the newly created variable and enter values for each case. Repeat for each desired variable and case to fill in your data. When you are

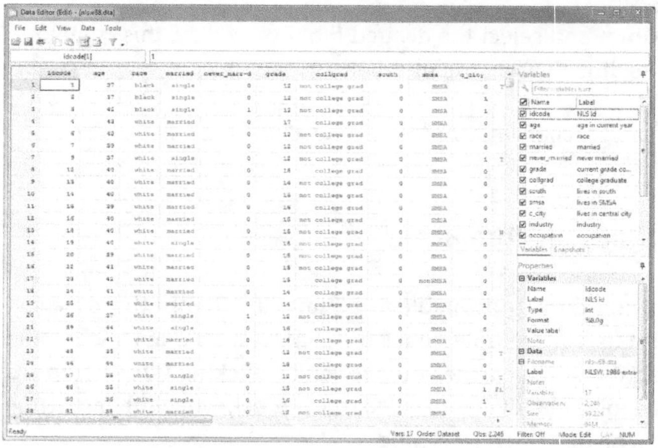

Figure 2.2: Stata's Data Editor.

done close the window. When you want to browse your data, which is a common task, to check whether data transformations were successful, it is better to use the browsing window, as there you cannot accidentally change data values. Just enter

```
browse
```

or click the **Data Editor (Browse)** button.

2.5 Using preinstalled data

One of the great advantages of Stata is that it comes with tons of tested and refined datasets that are preinstalled or available on the net. To see the available datasets, click **File → Example Datasets** and then *Example datasets installed with Stata*. Then click *use* to load the desired dataset. Throughout the book we will rely on preinstalled or online datasets as they are very easy to open and perfect for learning. For example, when you want to open auto.dta, you can also enter directly

```
sysuse auto
```

The dataset is opened into Stata. If there is already unsaved data in memory, you have to save or close it first in order to open the new file.

Installing community-contributed software

One of the greatest advantages of Stata is its flexibility. It happens quite often that statisticians develop a cool new method for data analyses. As Stata is released only every few years, and updates do not cover brand-new methods, users have the chance of writing their own little programs that can be integrated smoothly into Stata. These are called community-contributed software (CCS, informally also called *Ados*) and are extremely useful. You can even write your own CCS and share them on the Internet if you think some features are still missing! To search for new CCS click **Help → SJ and User-written Programs** and you will see some options.

When you have a special method in mind, that is missing in Stata, it is a good idea to search the Internet for it with Stata as a keyword, and useful results often show up quickly. Installing CCS sometimes just requires typing one command and you are done, others will come with a longer manual and tell you to download specific files. It is usually a good idea to use CCS that are already added to the official Stata database, so you know they are tested, trusted and safe to use. When you find such a CCS, for example *psmatch2*, a popular command for propensity score matching, you can type

```
ssc install psmatch2
```

Other information for using SPSS files: a CCS for importing is provided by Sergiy Radyakin (Windows only). You can check out his website[3] to learn how to install it.

2.6 Saving and exporting data

After you are done with your work you usually want to save your data. Two notes of caution. Firstly, never overwrite your original dataset as any changes you make are permanent! If you made an error there is no way to correct it later. Therefore, you should save the dataset with a new name. Secondly, it is usually a good idea to export your dataset to an open file format, after your project is finished. This makes it much easier for your colleagues and other researchers to open and handle your data in the future. A good option for doing this is saving as a .csv file, which can be opened on any computer, even without Stata. The biggest downside of these open formats is that all metadata is lost. Thus it is suggested to use different formats simultaneously when archiving your projects. Remember, exporting need not to be done in your daily work routine, but once you are finished, for archiving purposes.

To save your dataset, click **File → Save as** and choose the desired folder and name. The dialogue also makes it possible to save your files for older Stata versions. For example, version 12 cannot open files saved with Stata 15, so when some of your colleagues still use an older version you can set the option. If you want to use the command, type

---

3 http://www.radyakin.org/transfer/usespss/faq/usespss_faq.html (2018-01-16).

```
save "filename.dta"
```

Again, when you use this relative pathway, your file will be saved in the current working directory. To export your dataset, click **File → Export → Comma- or tab separated data** or type

```
export delimited "filename.csv"4
```

When exporting to text files, pay attention to how your non-integers are formatted. The exporting process will save these numbers with the displayed format; this may cause loss of precision. For more information on this issue type

```
help format
```

2.7 The basic workflow

Now you know how to open and save files, which means you can start managing and analyzing data. A few more words on the basic Stata workflow, beforehand, which will save you many hours of trouble in the future, as good routines and basic safety measures will make working with Stata so much better (I promise!).

First of all, as mentioned above, never ever overwrite or change your original dataset. Sometimes this can be a minor problem when the dataset is downloaded from the Internet and can be restored. In other cases, as with data that you personally put together, this might be impossible. Therefore, whenever you receive a new dataset: make a copy and archive it. A very convenient method is to use the built-in compressing function of your computer and save your data file as a "zipped" archive (for example as a .zip or .rar file) with the current date. By doing this, you always have a copy you cannot accidentally change as it is compressed.

After this, we can start with do-files, which will radically improve your workflow and make it easy and convenient to replicate what you did (for you and other people). Basically, a do-file is a plain text file that contains all commands you use to alter or analyze your dataset. When you come back later, maybe in some years, the do-file tells you what you did with your data in the first place, and makes it possible to replicate your previous findings. This is also crucial for science as a whole, as replicability of data analyses is important to tell other researchers how you came to your results. When needed, other researchers can reconstruct your analysis. This underlines how intersubjectivity can be reached. It still might be the case that other people do not agree with you on all details, as they might have chosen different variables or another

---

4 If this command does not work as you are using an older version, try *outsheet using "filename.csv"*

operationalization, yet you can document and justify your proceedings. Finally, when you come to the conclusion that you have had enough Stata for a day, and want to save your results, it is more common to save the do-files with all your commands than to save changes directly into a .dta file. Thus, you are strongly advised to use do-files every time when working with Stata. Although it might seem like extra work at first, after a week you will have internalized this good habit.

2.8 Do-files

Usually, the first thing you want to do after starting Stata is to get your do-file running. When you already have one, from the last session or from your colleagues, you can open it by clicking **Window → do-file editor → New do-file editor** or type

doedit

Figure 2.3: Stata's Do-file Editor.

A new window will appear (Figure 2.3). In that window, click **File → Open** and open the file. You can recognize do-files by the suffix .do. Otherwise you can just start by typing first commands in the empty do-file-Editor.

In my opinion, most do-files should start with these four lines[5]:

```
clear all              //clear memory
version 15             //your current version
capture log close      //close any log-files
set more off           //do not halt
```

The first line (clear all) removes any datasets, saved variables, macros or loops from the memory. This means you get a fresh start and have the system ready to work. Of course, before running the code make sure that you have saved all your current datasets, otherwise the data will be lost!

The second line (version 15) tells Stata which version you are currently running. This is important for archiving purposes. Now suppose you used Stata 10 in the past, but then you switched to the newest version and some command syntax was changed in the meantime. If you ran your old do-file from version 10 in Stata 15, your old do-file might not work, and produce an error message instead. Although this is rarely the case, it is good practice to include this line. You can see your current version directly on the output screen after Stata has started (or just type *version*).

The third line (capture log close) checks whether an active log-file is running. If so, it will close it.[6] For more information about logs see page 12.

The last line (set more off) is useful for long do-files that should run without any interruption, and is especially important when you are not running version 15 or newer. Some commands produce a lot of output and older versions will halt, so the user can check it. You can either hit the space bar or click "Show more" to see the next few lines of output. As this gets tiring after a while, automatically showing all lines is quite convenient.

You may have also noticed the comments after the commands shown above. When working with do-files, it is highly recommended that you comment on (some) commands. Later, they will be useful to help you remember what you did. To write a comment after a command just type two slashes (//). Any character in the same line after them will be ignored by Stata. When you need comments that stretch over several lines, use

```
/* This is a long comment that
   will take several lines and
   is probably not very useful */
```

---

5 When entering commands from this book, you do not have to type the comments which start with //. These are only in the book to help you understand what is going on, and always ignored by Stata when running commands.

6 The command *capture* can be used in combination with any other command. If the second command fails and produces an error, Stata then ignores this and continues with the rest of the code. Therefore, using capture always requires caution.

The indentation of the second and third line is not required, but might improve readability. You will also notice that Stata changes the color for comments so they are even more clear to the user. It is also a good idea to use headlines and sub-headlines to structure your do-files. Starting a line with an asterisk (*) will do this for you. As a general rule, it is a good idea to comment on complex parts of the code that will help you remember how they work. Simple commands like opening or saving files do not deserve comments in real files, as this might clutter your do-file and affect readability.

By the way, when you have a really long command in your do-file, you can use a triple slash (///). Just continue your command in the next line, for example

```
drop if age < 40 & sex == 1 & income > 4000 ///
    & BMI > 28 & wave == 5[7]
```

This is useful for readability, but Stata does not care how many characters are in one line.

Now you can start with actual work, by opening the desired file. You can either type the command to open the file in the command line directly and hit Enter, or you can type it into the do-file, or you can use point-and-click. When you typed it into the do-file, you will notice that nothing has happened yet. You have to execute the command so Stata will start working. You can do this by selecting the desired line(s) or all lines in the do-file with the mouse, then enter **Ctrl + D**. Alternatively, click **Tools → Execute (do)**. You do not have to select the desired line(s) entirely, but at least one character in each line has to be selected. If zero characters are selected, Stata will run the entire do-file from top to bottom. When you look at your output window, you will see that Stata opened the desired file. When you use point-and-click Stata will automatically create the command that runs "behind the scenes" and save it in the Review window. It is always a good idea to inspect these commands to see how Stata works.

To summarize it, you basically have three options to save your commands using do-files:
- Type all commands in the do-file directly and run them from there.
- Type all commands in the interactive Command line and after the command was run successfully, right-click on the command in the history-window and copy-paste it into your do-file.
- Type all commands in the interactive Command line and let Stata copy them automatically into the file. The advantage of this method is that you do not have to do it manually afterwards; the problem is that misspecified commands, say

---

[7] If you want to know more about the double equal sign, see page 31.

with a typo, will be copied so you later have to come back and control what you did. If you prefer this third option, type

```
cmdlog using "filename.do", append
```

Stata will create a new file called *filename.do* or, if it already exists, append all new commands to the end of it.

Congratulations! By reaching this point, you have mastered the first part of the book. Now you know how to open, save and manage your files. You are ready to start some real data manipulation in the next chapter!

2.9 Delimit and line breaks*

When using do-files, Stata expects one command per line. You can create longer commands by using three backslashes (///), yet even this solution can be problematic when dealing with very long commands. Especially when recoding variables with several categories or creating sophisticated graphs, many lines will be needed. To avoid a structure using backslashes, Stata offers the possibility of using a semicolon (;) as an artificial line break set by the user. Any other line breaks will be ignored until Stata reaches a semicolon. To do this, type in your do-file[8]:

```
#delimit ;
//your very long command goes here;
#delimit cr
```

Until the *#delimit cr* part is reached, Stata will only see ends of lines when reaching a semicolon. Some users prefer to use this option as a default. The problem is that forgetting a semicolon at the end of a command will mess your code up.

Log-Files and folder structures

When you remember the do-file code from page 12, you will notice a line about Log-Files. Logs can be useful when you have really long do-files, that produce a lot of output (for example your results in the form of tables) and run for a long time, sometimes hours or even days (no kidding!). In this case, you don't want to wait in front of the computer and copy all the output you receive from the Results-Window. Log-Files are a convenient tool, to write every output to a text file which you can later open

---

8 This command will actually work *only* in a do-file and not when typed directly into the command window.

in Stata or any text editor. This information will also be available if Stata or your computer crashes. Finally, this can be really helpful when it comes to replication purposes. I do not advise using Log-Files for every single small output you produce, but rather for larger chunks of your work, so that you can put these in an archive.

To start a Log-File, add this line to the top of your do-file:

```
log using "logname.log", name(log1)
```

The name option allows you to name the current Log-File, which is always a good idea and makes nested logging possible. When you already have an existing Log-File that you want to overwrite, add the option *replace*

```
log using "logname.log", name(log1) replace
```

When you want to extend the existing Log-File without overwriting the older data, use the option *append* instead. At the end of your do-file put the line

```
log close log1
```

to terminate the logging. The Log-File will be created in your current working directory. You can also create and manage Log-Files in the GUI by clicking **File → Log → Begin...**

For large projects, like a seminar paper or a thesis, you will clearly have an extra folder on your computer. Within this, creating four Stata folders is often useful.

Data contains all your data files, like raw data or .dta files
Do contains all do-files that you created
Log contains all Log-Files Stata created for you
Graph contains all graphics and figures you created with Stata

By doing this, it will be easier for you to find the correct file faster and have a better view of your project. Over time you will develop your own system to manage your data.

3 Cleaning and preparing data

As you are familiar with the basic steps for working with Stata, we will focus on real data editing and work through some examples. In this chapter, we will start to prepare data. Over time you will see that running actual statistical methods is often done very quickly, yet cleaning and preparing data, so you can use it for your desired methods, will take the lion's share of your time.

3.1 Getting to know your data

Suppose you get a new dataset for the very first time, maybe from your colleagues, a research institute or a government agency. In the best case, there exists information about how the data was collected, generated and processed. Then it is a great idea to first study these documents, so you know what you are working with. As we are realists, we assume there is no documentation, and we have to find out the important stuff alone. In this chapter we will use a preinstalled dataset from the National Longitudinal Survey that contains information about the working careers of women in their thirties and forties. The data was collected in the USA in 1988. We start with a fresh Stata window and open the dataset by typing

```
sysuse nlsw88, clear
```

Sysuse opens a preinstalled ("system") dataset, *nlsw88* is the name of the specific dataset, and the option *clear* tells Stata to delete any loaded data in memory, if there is any.[1]

  The best idea is to get a rough overview of the data, so we see which variables are contained and what they are about. Try

```
describe
```

or click **Data → Describe data → Describe data in memory or in a file**. Another tip: when you want to see the dialogue box but do not want to click through the entire menu tree, just type *db*, followed by the command of interest (for example: *db describe*).

  We get a large amount of information. There are 2,246 *obs* (observations, cases) in the file. 17 *vars* (variables) are contained in the dataset which are listed separately below. *Size* tells us how large the dataset is (about 60kb).

  Now to the details about the variables. *Variable name* tells us the name of the variable (duh!). Note that some of them seem quite obvious (wage), while others

---

1 If you want to see all available preinstalled datasets on your computer, type *sysuse dir*.

https://doi.org/10.1515/9783110617160-003

```
Contains data from C:\Program Files (x86)\Stata15\ado\base/n/nlsw88.dta
  obs:          2,246                      NLSW, 1988 extract
  vars:            17                      1 May 2016 22:52
  size:        60,642                      (_dta has notes)
```

	storage	display	value	
variable name	type	format	label	variable label
idcode	int	%8.0g		NLS id
age	byte	%8.0g		age in current year
race	byte	%8.0g	racelbl	race
married	byte	%8.0g	marlbl	married
never_married	byte	%8.0g		never married
grade	byte	%8.0g		current grade completed
collgrad	byte	%16.0g	gradlbl	college graduate
south	byte	%8.0g		lives in south
smsa	byte	%9.0g	smsalbl	lives in SMSA
c_city	byte	%8.0g		lives in central city
industry	byte	%23.0g	indlbl	industry
occupation	byte	%22.0g	occlbl	occupation
union	byte	%8.0g	unionlbl	union worker
wage	float	%9.0g		hourly wage
hours	byte	%8.0g		usual hours worked
ttl_exp	float	%9.0g		total work experience
tenure	float	%9.0g		job tenure (years)

Sorted by: idcode

are rather cryptic (ttl_exp). To find out what this means, we can look at the *variable label*, which contains a description of each variable. It is usually a good idea to keep variable names short and concise, as they are often typed and should not clutter our code. Still, they should be meaningful and tell us roughly what they are about. Longer descriptions can go with the variable labels, which are especially helpful for people who are new to the dataset. For the moment we can safely ignore *storage type* and *display format*. Lastly, we see that some variables have an entry under value label, others do not. This basically tells us whether the values of the variable are named (labeled). We will deal with these aspects of data management in the following sections. The next figure (Figure 3.1) will help you to understand what these are all about.

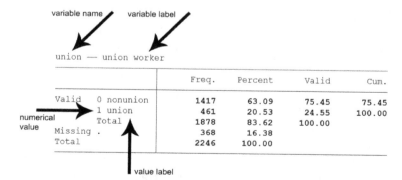

Figure 3.1: Variable name, label, values and value labels.

Listing cases

Sometimes you see strange behavior in your data and want to look at certain cases that might contain wrong or unusual data. You can do this by using the Data Editor window which might be a good idea when your dataset is small. When you have thousands of cases and hundreds of variables, this might not help you. A possible solution is the *list* command that helps you inspecting interesting cases. For example, when we want to see the properties of respondents younger than 40, that are from the south and union members, we type

```
list if age < 40 & south == 1 & union == 1
```

108.	idcode	age	race	married	never_~d	grade	collgrad	south	smsa	c_city
	257	38	black	married	0	16	college grad	1	SMSA	1

	industry		occupation		union	wage	hours	ttl_exp	tenure
	Professional Services		Professional/technical		union	11.6103	40	11.65385	2.75

138.	idcode	age	race	married	never_~d	grade	collgrad	south	smsa	c_city
	325	34	white	single	1	12	not college grad	1	SMSA	0

	industry		occupation		union	wage	hours	ttl_exp	tenure
	Transport/Comm/Utility		Laborers		union	4.613526	60	16.11539	3.25

–Further output omitted-

or click **Data → Describe data → List data.** You will receive a list that contains all information for all cases that fit the condition. If you just want to have a general look at your data, type

```
list in 1/10
```

– output omitted -

The "in" part means that only the first 10 observations will be shown to you, otherwise the list might be a little long! Note that you can always stop Stata producing output by pressing Q. You can also combine *in* and *if* in the same command

```
list idcode age grade union wage in 1/10 if age < 40
```

	idcode	age	grade	union	wage
1.	1	37	12	union	11.73913
2.	2	37	12	union	6.400963
6.	7	39	12	nonunion	4.62963
7.	9	37	12	union	10.49114

3.2 Variable names and labels

Each variable has a unique name and a label (which should be unique as well). Whenever you use or manipulate a variable, you have to use the variable name. To change variable names or labels we click **Data → Variables Manager.** There we see a list of all existing variables, their names, labels and corresponding value labels. This is a great tool for managing the most basic properties of our variables. Suppose we want to rename the variable smsa to metro and change the variable label:

```
rename smsa metro
label variable metro "Standard Metropolitan Statistical Area"
```

The command *label variable,* allows you to change the label of the variable metro to any text you put in quotation marks directly after. In general, it is strongly advised to label your variables so you know immediately what they are about.

3.3 Labeling values

Momentarily, all information in the dataset is in numerical form (that means there is no text data like names or strings). Each variable can take certain values, which are coded as numbers. Some variables are binary (only two values are possible, such as, 0 and 1). Examples are gender (male and female) or marital status (married and not married). As it might be hard to remember whether 0 or 1 stands for "married", we can label our values. By doing this Stata will remember for us the correct specification. Note that the label per se is only useful for us humans as the computer always uses numbers to compute results mathematically. Luckily, most values are labeled already. This really helps us knowing which number stands for which answer given by the participants. Only the variable c_city lacks a value label. From the description, we learn that this variable tells us whether a participant lives in a "central city" (whatever this means).

To get more information about this variable, we will inspect it by typing

```
tabulate c_city
```

lives in central city	Freq.	Percent	Cum.
0	1,591	70.84	70.84
1	655	29.16	100.00
Total	2,246	100.00	

We see that 655 persons are coded with 1, which we assume means "yes". Now we want to label these values. To do this in Stata, we will have to use two steps.
1. Create a *value label* and give it a name.
2. Tell Stata to use the generated value label for the desired variable(s).

We create a value label by clicking **Data → Data Utilities → Label Utilities → Manage value labels**. A new window will pop up that lists all existing value labels. By clicking all little arrows we can make sure that none of the existing labels corresponds to a no – yes labeling. Therefore, we click **Create Label**. We call our new label "yesno" and enter the values, 0 with "no", 1 with "yes". Then we click **OK** and see that our label is in the list. Now we can tell Stata to use this label for our variable c_city. We close the window and click **Data → Data Utilities → Label Utilities → Assign label value to variables**. In the new window we enter the name of your variable (c_city) under Variables, or click the little arrow to choose it from the list. Under Value Label we choose yesno and click **OK**. Another way to do it is to use the **properties window**. Make sure to click the padlock icon to unlock the window, so you can enter information.

We can check our results by typing

```
tabulate c_city
```

```
   lives in
    central
       city │     Freq.      Percent        Cum.
────────────┼───────────────────────────────────
         no │     1,591        70.84       70.84
        yes │       655        29.16      100.00
────────────┼───────────────────────────────────
      Total │     2,246       100.00
```

For beginners, this process might seem tedious, as we first have to create a new label and tell Stata to use it with our variable. The major advantage is that by doing so, we could label a lot of "yes – no" questions at the same time! Imagine we had information on whether people like Pizza Hawaii, drive a Porsche or ever went bungee jumping. All these questions can be answered in a binary fashion and, when they have the same numerical values, we can label them all at once.

To do the process described above with commands, we type

```
label define yesno 1 "yes" 0 "no"
label values c_city yesno
```

Which workflow you prefer is up to you. Most people will switch from the point-and-click method to commands as soon as they are more familiar with them. We want to copy these commands to our do-file, which is hopefully already running and has a nice header (when you have absolutely no idea what I am talking about, have a look at page 12). To do this, hold **Ctrl** and click the corresponding commands in the Review window on the left side of the screen. Then, right-click one of them and click **Copy**. Now you can paste them into your do-file, so they are saved. Maybe later we learn that 1 actually means "no" and 0 actually means "yes". Then we can go back and correct our mistake easily.

By the way, which variables should have value labels? "Categorical variables should have labels, unless the variable has an inherent metric" (Long, 2009: 163). Examples of variables with inherent metric are age, income or time spent watching TV per day in minutes.

3.4 IDs and unique identifiers

Many datasets contain one case (person) per row, especially when we talk about cross-sectional data (that is when all data entries are from the same point in time, e.g. the same year). Every person should have a unique identifier, which is often a number or a code. If there are identifiers in our list that are not unique, which means that several persons have the same ID, we have a problem. In Stata it is easy to test whether an ID is unique. Click **Data → Data Utilities → Check for unique identifiers** and select the ID variable (idcode). Or use the command

```
isid idcode
```

As we do not receive any error message, the assumption is fulfilled. When no unique ID exists, but we are absolutely sure that there are no duplicates in our dataset, we can create it. Try typing

```
generate ID = _n
label variable ID "new unique identifier"
```

This will create a new variable ID that gives each person a number, starting with 1. _n is a system variable which tells Stata the position (going from 1 up to the last observation) of each case in the dataset. Another helpful system variable is _N which is the total number of observations in your dataset. You can inspect the results using the data browser. When you are not sure if any duplicates exist in your data, click **Data → Data Utilities → Manage duplicate observations** or type

```
duplicates list idcode-tenure
```

The part idcode-tenure, tells Stata to use all variables in the dataset, except the newly created ID variable. To see how this works, take a look at the variable window.

The variables are in a certain order and new ones are created at the bottom of the list. The hyphen tells Stata to use all variables from idcode to tenure, but not ID, which is below tenure. As ID *must* differ across all cases, by design, we should not use it in our duplicates test. Luckily, our dataset seems to be fine.

Note that you can also create IDs separately for subgroups in the data. Imagine we want to create different IDs within the industry where a person works. Try:

```
bysort industry: generate ind_ID = _n
```

This command will first sort all cases by industry, and then start enumerating persons within each industry from 1 until all persons have a number. When it reaches the next industry, it will start, again, from 1 and label all persons. Suppose you want to mark the youngest person in each industry. Try:

```
bysort industry (age): generate age_ID = _n
list industry age age_ID in 1/20
```

	industry	age	age_ID
1.	Ag/Forestry/Fisheries	34	1
2.	Ag/Forestry/Fisheries	35	2
3.	Ag/Forestry/Fisheries	36	3
4.	Ag/Forestry/Fisheries	37	4
5.	Ag/Forestry/Fisheries	38	5
6.	Ag/Forestry/Fisheries	39	6
7.	Ag/Forestry/Fisheries	40	7
8.	Ag/Forestry/Fisheries	40	8
9.	Ag/Forestry/Fisheries	40	9
10.	Ag/Forestry/Fisheries	40	10
11.	Ag/Forestry/Fisheries	41	11
12.	Ag/Forestry/Fisheries	42	12
13.	Ag/Forestry/Fisheries	42	13
14.	Ag/Forestry/Fisheries	43	14
15.	Ag/Forestry/Fisheries	43	15
16.	Ag/Forestry/Fisheries	44	16
17.	Ag/Forestry/Fisheries	45	17
18.	Mining	35	1
19.	Mining	35	2
20.	Mining	36	3

What Stata does here is first sort all cases by industry, and, within industry, by age. Putting age in parentheses will prevent Stata from creating several counters within each industry, using age as a second hierarchy. To see how this works in detail, play around with the commands to become more familiar with them. You can also sort variables into ascending order by values, without creating variables using the sort command:

```
sort age              //Sort cases by age (ascending)
sort married age      //Sort by marriage-status and within groups by age
```

If you want to reverse the order (sort in descending order) use *gsort*:

```
gsort -age            //Sort cases by age (descending)
```

Using the Stata documentation

One of the greatest strengths of Stata is its excellent documentation, which comprises more than 14,000 pages. Clearly, even more experienced users will not remember every single option for all commands. Stata knows this and tries to help. Whenever you want to learn more about a command just type *help* and the name of the command in the command line, for example

```
help generate
```

Figure 3.2: Stata's internal documentation system.

A new window will pop up that contains a large amount of information (Figure 3.2). As these help files always follow the same structure, I want to give a short explanation here.

Before the text even begins, have a look at the three small fields in the upper right corner which you can click. "Dialog" opens the point-and-click interface of the respective command whose help-file you just studied (if available). "Also see" links you to other help-files for similar commands which might be relevant as well, so clicking there is often a great idea. Finally, "Jump to", lets you navigate quickly through the current help file, which is a boon for longer ones.

Now to the main part of the help-file. The first section contains a generic example to see how this command should be used (the syntax). This is often helpful, as it tells you where each part of the command goes and how the command is structured. Everything in brackets [...] is optional, meaning that these parts are not needed to run the command. The next thing you see is the pathway to point-and-click, which is available for the vast majority of all commands. After that, a more detailed explanation of the command follows, which tells you what the command can do and how it is best used.

Then the options are explained, which can customize the way the command works. More experienced statistical methods often have dozens of options, so it is usually a good idea to browse this section when using a command for the first time (also have a look at the point-and-click interface, as this is often more convenient). After that, several examples with real (online) data are presented, which you can use to practice right, away and see the command in action. This is great when you do not have suitable data available and just want to get to know the methods. Some commands like *regress* will also show a section about saved results which we will explain later (see page 49). The help file usually ends with references, which tell you which algorithms were used and where they are documented. Using the Stata helpfiles is a great way to improve your knowledge and explore the wide range of possibilities Stata offers. Always remember that you do not have to memorize every single bit of a command as the help file will provide the information when needed.

3.5 Missing values

Missing data is a widespread problem in any empirical research. In the social sciences, people often do not want to answer certain questions or some statistics are not available for all countries in the political sciences. You have to tell Stata that a certain numerical value should be interpreted as a missing value, otherwise you run into problems. Stata uses the dot (.) to depict missing values. Type

```
misstable summarize, all
```

or click **Statistics → Summaries, tables and tests → Tables → Tabulate missing values,** then click *Show all variables* and click *OK*. You will see a table that displays for each variable how many missings they include. The variable *union* seems to be especially problematic, as 368 people refused to answer this question. So we do not know whether they are in a union or not.

Somehow we are still lucky because Stata automatically recognizes that some cases do not have information. Suppose we get data from a colleague who coded all missing values with the numerical value -999. Stata would not know that these values are not normal numerical values, that should be handled differently. This is why inspecting our dataset in the first place is so crucial. The table we have just produced also contains a column for Min and Max values, which is very helpful in this case.

			Obs<.	Obs<.		
Variable	Obs=.	Obs>.	Obs<.	Unique values	Min	Max
idcode			2,246	>500	1	5159
age			2,246	13	34	46
race			2,246	3	1	3
married			2,246	2	0	1
never_marr~d			2,246	2	0	1
grade	2		2,244	16	0	18
collgrad			2,246	2	0	1
south			2,246	2	0	1
smsa			2,246	2	0	1
c_city			2,246	2	0	1
industry	14		2,232	12	1	12
occupation	9		2,237	13	1	13
union	368		1,878	2	0	1
wage			2,246	>500	1.004952	40.74659
hours	4		2,242	62	1	80
ttl_exp			2,246	>500	.1153846	28.88461
tenure	15		2,231	259	0	25.91667
ID			2,246	>500	1	2246
ind_ID			2,246	>500	1	824

Yet at first glance, all values seem *plausible*. This is also true for other variables like age, where values below zero or above 100 should also make us think!

To tell Stata which value labels stand for missings (in this hypothetical case -999) we use the following command:

```
replace VAR =. if VAR == -999
```

where VAR stands for the name of the variable we want to change. Also note that Stata offers a convenient tool to change these missing codes for several variables at a time. This comes in handy when you know an institute uses the same numerical values for all variables to declare missings. Try

```
mvdecode _all, mv(-999)                    //Change -999 to .
```

You can also reverse this and turn all missing values (.) back into plain numerical values. Try

```
mvencode _all, mv(-999)                    //Change . to -999
```

or click **Data → Create or change data → Other variable-transformation commands → Change missing values to numeric**.

Another word of caution: although missing values are depicted with a dot in Stata, they still have an internal numerical representation. Actually, Stata uses the

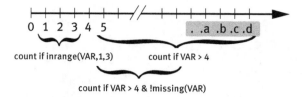

Figure 3.3: Stata's internal representation of missing values.

largest possible numerical value to indicate missings. This can be a great source of problems if one forgets about this. Suppose we wanted to compare values and count how many people work more than 60 hours a week. We would enter

```
count if hours > 60²
```

The displayed result is 22, which is incorrect, as four of these persons have missing values, and should thus not be counted at all. To resolve this problem we have to type

```
count if hours > 60 & !missing(hours)
```

You can also do this in the GUI by clicking **Data → Data Utilities → Count observations satisfying condition**. To visualize how Stata handles missing values, have a look at Figure 3.3.

Note that you can also have distinct missing values that can be used to give more information about the type of missing value (extended missing values). When collecting data there are several possibilities why data is missing: the respondent was not home, he refused to answer the question and so on. To code these, try

```
replace VAR = .a if VAR == -99        //Not home
replace VAR = .b if VAR == -999       //Refusal
replace VAR = .c if VAR == -9999      //Implausible value
```

Stata will count all numerical values that start with a dot followed by exactly one letter as missings and will not use them in any statistic it computes.

3.6 Creating new variables

Finally, we come to the fun part where we create our own new variables. Creating variables might be at the heart of data preparation, as data is rarely in the form we want it to be when we receive it. Luckily, the general scheme for doing this is very easy. We still have our NLSW88 dataset open. As you can see we have one variable age which

---

2 To learn more about the if qualifier, have a look at page 30.

tells us how old participants are at the time of the survey in 1988. Let's suppose we want a variable that tells us not the age, but the year of birth of the person. The year of birth is just the year of survey minus age, thus we type

```
generate ybirth = 1988-age
```

Alternatively, click **Data → Create or change data → Create new variable**, enter the name of the new variable (ybirth) and the expression to generate it (1988-age), then click OK. When we click in the variable window (top right) and scroll down, we can see that the variable was actually generated, congratulations! Yet the variable label is still missing so we type

```
label variable ybirth "Year of birth"
```

We can control our result by typing

```
tabulate ybirth
```

ybirth	Freq.	Percent	Cum.
1942	2	0.09	0.09
1943	78	3.47	3.56
1944	163	7.26	10.82
1945	165	7.35	18.17
1946	160	7.12	25.29
1947	222	9.88	35.17
1948	208	9.26	44.43
1949	234	10.42	54.85
1950	219	9.75	64.60
1951	225	10.02	74.62
1952	257	11.44	86.06
1953	260	11.58	97.64
1954	53	2.36	100.00
Total	2,246	100.00	

or click **Statistics → Summaries, tables and tests → Tables → One-way tables** and enter *ybirth* under *Categorical variable* and click OK. As you see, the general way of generating variables is easy. You use the *generate* command, specify the name of the new variable, type the equal sign, and then the expression you would like to have.

Let's take another example. Imagine we want to generate the squared version of age. Someone with an age of 30 should thus have a value of $30^2 = 900$. To do this we type

```
generate age_squared = age^2
```

Please check whether the result is correct, and label the variable in a useful fashion.

Generating variables is a powerful command that enables you to manipulate data in many ways, as you can use a lot of mathematical operators or other functions. You can receive a list of the possibilities by using the GUI, as described above, or type

```
help functions
```

As a side note: when typing commands directly into Stata, you can use the tabulator key for auto-completion. This can be highly useful when dealing with long or cryptic variable names: type the first few characters of the variable name, and hit tab. As long as the name is unambiguous, Stata will show the complete name of the variable.

3.6.1 Special functions

Stata comes with a long list of functions that make generating new variables easy and comfortable. I want to present a small outline, as they are useful in daily routines.

Inlist
Inlist can be used to test for certain conditions instead, of using a long command with a lot of "or" options (the vertical bar). Compare the following commands, as they do the same thing:

```
count if occupation == 1 | occupation == 2 | ///
      occupation == 3 | occupation == 4
count if inlist(occupation,1,2,3,4)
```

Another trick is to use the first argument not for the name of a variable, but with a numerical value to find all cases that have at least one matching condition.

```
count if inlist(1,union,south,c_city)
```

which is equal to

```
count if union == 1 | south == 1 | c_city == 1
```

Inrange
Inrange gives you all cases that fall within a certain range. Suppose that we want all women that earn between 10 and 15 dollars per hour (including both limits):

```
count if inrange(wage,10,15)
```

which is the same as the longer command

```
count if wage ≥10 & wage ≤15
```

Of course you can use a *generate* command instead of the *count* when needed.

Autocode

When we do not want to explicitly state the size of each category in a recode transformation, we can use *autocode*. As long as we tell Stata how many categories we want in total, it will automatically form them with equal sizes (not equal number of cases!). When we want to have a variable with five categories about tenure, try

```
generate tenure_cat = autocode(tenure,5,0,27)
tabulate tenure_cat   //Inspect results
```

tenure_cat	Freq.	Percent	Cum.
5.4	1,307	58.58	58.58
10.8	492	22.05	80.64
16.2	278	12.46	93.10
21.6	142	6.36	99.46
27	12	0.54	100.00
Total	2,231	100.00	

Tenure is the name of the variable we want to recode, 5 is the number of categories we want, 0 is the smallest value that should be considered in the recode and 27 is the largest value. It is usually a good idea to inspect the Min and Max of the variable we recode, and then use these values. Note that this command works best with integers. If your original variable includes decimal numbers, make sure to inspect the result carefully as the border categories might have an unequal size.

When you want to use point-and-click to use these advanced functions, click **Data → Create of change data → Create new variable**, tick *Specify a value or an expression* and click *Create*. Then click *Functions* and choose *Programming*. You will see a large list with short descriptions of each command.

Egen

The *generate* command has a slightly more advanced brother, the *egen* command. Using different suboptions, *egen* offers several dozens of ways to manipulate data. When you want to create a new variable, that contains for each case the maximum value of some other variables, you can use this. Imagine we want to know, for each woman, where she has the largest value: wage, tenure or hour? We type

```
egen maxvalue = rowmax(wage tenure hours)
sort idcode
list idcode maxvalue wage tenure hours in 1/10
```

	idcode	maxvalue	wage	tenure	hours
1.	2546	40	8.05153	13.5	40
2.	4053	50	11.15941	12.66667	50
3.	195	40	4.53301	2.166667	40
4.	460	3.099125	3.099125	1.5	3
5.	1201	50	6.191625	2.5	50
6.	1588	24	4.025765	.1666667	24
7.	4184	40	12.38325	17.66667	40
8.	4838	50	2.508361	.4166667	50
9.	3059	10.62802	10.62802	1.333333	7
10.	4995	26	7.589398	2.333333	26

Note that this example is somewhat artificial, as usually the variables you want to compare, in this way, should use the same metric.

You can also get the minimum (rowmin), mean (rowmean), median (rowmedian) or the number of missings (rowmiss). The last option is especially helpful when you want to select all cases that have complete information on all desired variables.

To use *egen* with point-and-click, go **Data → Create or change data → Create new variable (extended)**.

3.7 The if qualifier

If (!) you have a background in programming you will be familiar with if conditions that are used to structure program flow and to process data selectively. The basic idea is that Stata should do action X if and only if condition Y is true. This is one of the most central aspects of data managing, as it allows you to change properties of variables in many ways. For example, when we want to know how many people are in our dataset that are younger than 30 and union members, we use the *count* command. When we use this command without any if qualifiers, it will just count how many cases are in our dataset (2,246). Now we combine *count* and the if qualifier, to count only the cases where the condition is true:

```
count if age < 35 & union == 1
```

The "&" means "and" in Stata. To form more complex conditions, you can use these operators (see Table 3.1):

Table 3.1: Logical operators in Stata.

Operator	Meaning	Operator	Meaning
&	and	>	greater than
|[3]	or (nonexclusive)	<	less than
!	not (equal)/negation	≥	greater than or equal
==	equal	≤	less than or equal

Parentheses are also important helpers to structure conditions. As you might remember from math class, parentheses bind stronger than other operators and often make a difference. Here are some examples:

Older or exactly 40 years old and married:

```
count if age ≥ 40 & !missing(age) & married == 1⁴
```

Working in mining or construction and not white:

```
count if (industry == 2 | industry == 3) & race != 1 ///
    & !missing(race)
```

Younger than 35 and income larger or equal to 25 (and also not counting missing values):

```
count if age < 35 & wage ≥ 25 & !missing(wage)
```

If qualifiers are super important and can be combined with most Stata commands. To check whether you can use an if qualifier in combination with another command, refer to the documentation (for more information see page 23). Further, make sure that the values you compare have no missing values, or at least consider this possibility (as in the first example shown above), otherwise results might be incorrect (which is explained on page 26).

Assigning VS equality testing

You have probably asked yourself by now why sometimes you need = and sometimes you need ==. The explanation is that they imply a different thing. The single version means that you assign a certain value to a variable, while the double version tests for equality. Explained differently, the single version

---

3 This character is called *Sheffer stroke* or just vertical bar. Typing it might involve using the Shift key or the AltGr key, depending on your keyboard layout.
4 The condition & *!missing(age)* ensures that people with missing values on the variable age will not fulfill the condition and are, therefore, not counted. If you explicitly want to count people who have missings use & *missing(age)*.

represents "Stata, create this variable X here and set it to the value of Y!". The second version means "Stata, can you tell me whether this variable M here is equal to the value of N?". After a week of using Stata, this difference will be the most normal thing for you. Still, even experienced users sometimes forget one equal sign, which messes the code up. So always make sure to double check whether you really typed what you wanted.

3.8 Changing and replacing variables

Generating new variables is important, but often you still want to make changes to them later. As a general rule, never change existing (original) variables, in place, as these changes overwrite original data which could be a problem. It is a good habit to create new variables first from existing ones, and then change these newly created variables. If something goes wrong you still have the original in place and do not have to load a backup of your dataset.

Have a look at the variable, hours, which tells us how long participants work per week on average. This is a variable with an inherent metric as time in hours is a metric measurement. Assume we want to create an indicator that tells us whether a person works part-time, which is 20 hours or less. All persons working more than that will be counted as full-time workers. We want to create a binary indicator from this metric. First, we generate a new variable which we call "parttime".

```
generate parttime = .
```

This creates a variable that has missings for all cases which seems not very useful at first glance. Yet this is usually a good idea, as, if you make a mistake and your changes do not work, you will later see that many values are missing, which should alert you.

Before changing a variable, we have to think about how we want to operationalize (code) it. We decide that every person that works part-time will receive the value 1 (think of "yes") and all other persons will receive the value 0 ("no"). Now we can make the changes

```
replace parttime = 1 if hours ≤ 20
replace parttime = 0 if hours > 20 & !missing(hours)
tabulate parttime, missing
```

parttime	Freq.	Percent	Cum.
0	1,994	88.78	88.78
1	248	11.04	99.82
.	4	0.18	100.00
Total	2,246	100.00	

Alternatively, click **Data → Create or change data → Change contents of variable**. The option *missing* in the third command tells Stata to further display the information for cases with missing data (displayed with a dot symbol, 4 cases), which is often a good idea. Especially when working with expressions like "greater" or "smaller", it often happens that some cases at the borders can fall through the cracks. To avoid this, always think carefully before using the command and have safety checks afterward. A good way of doing this is by creating a crosstab or contingency table which displays the relations between two or more variables. In Stata we can do this by typing

tab̲ulate hours parttime, missing

usual hours worked	parttime 0	parttime 1	.	Total
1	0	1	0	1
2	0	7	0	7
3	0	5	0	5
4	0	6	0	6
5	0	7	0	7
6	0	2	0	2
7	0	5	0	5
8	0	12	0	12
9	0	4	0	4
10	0	15	0	15
11	0	1	0	1
12	0	10	0	10
13	0	1	0	1
14	0	2	0	2
15	0	40	0	40
16	0	21	0	21
17	0	3	0	3
18	0	11	0	11
20	0	95	0	95
21	3	0	0	3
22	8	0	0	8
23	7	0	0	7
24	36	0	0	36

– Rest of table omitted -

You will get a long output with all values. As you can see, all participants with 20 hours working time, or less, are in the right column under 1, while all others are in the left column. We can conclude from this that our new variable was created correctly. Another option for checking errors, that relies less on visual inspection of the tables, is the *assert* command. For example, we noticed that our variable used for generating parttime, hours, has four missing values. Therefore, our new variable should also include exactly four missing values. To check this we can use the following command:

```
assert missing(hours) == missing(parttime)
```

When this command runs without any errors, the condition is true. Otherwise Stata will halt and report that something you asserted is not correct.

Please label the new variable, and when you want, you can also apply the "yesno" label we created earlier[5] (see page 19).

New variables and labels in one step

When you have to change many variables, the process of creating them and labeling their values can be tiring. Luckily Stata offers a command to create variables, recode (change) them and label their values at the same time.

Let's have a look at the variable race which tells us the ethnic group of the participant. The categories are white, black and other. When we want to do a study about discrimination, we possibly need only two categories, white and non-white. So it would be a good idea to create a new variable that has the value 0 for all non-white persons and the value 1 for all white persons. First we have to find out how the existing variable is coded, which is done by typing

```
codebook race
```

---

race

---

type:	numeric (**byte**)		
label:	**racelbl**		
range:	[1,3]	units:	**1**
unique values:	3	missing .:	**0/2,246**
tabulation:	Freq.	Numeric	Label
	1,637	1	white
	583	2	black
	26	3	other

or click **Data → Describe data → Describe data contents (codebook)**.

There we see that 1 is coded for white, 2 for black and 3 for other. As we now know this, we can create a new variable by typing

```
recode race (1 = 1 "yes") (2 3 = 0 "no"), generate(is_white)
```

or click **Data → Create or change data → Other variable-transformation commands → Recode categorical variable**. Again we should crosscheck our results by typing

```
tabulate race is_white
```

---

5 As the label is already created, you only have to use the second command.

race	RECODE of race (race)		Total
	"no"	"yes"	
white	0	1,637	1,637
black	583	0	583
other	26	0	26
Total	609	1,637	2,246

Please note that the option *generate(is_white)* is crucial, otherwise your existing variable will be over-written! As the *recode* command is very helpful, it is a good idea to explore the many options available by typing

```
help recode
```

3.9 Removing observations and variables

Sometimes you want to remove observations from your dataset because they contain missing or wrong information. When you apply the following commands, make sure to save your dataset before, as we will not save the changes after removing observations and variables.

First, let's have a look at the variable grade which tells us how many years of schooling participants received. We will notice that there are a few cases that had less than four years of schooling, which is really short, and uncommon. We think that this might be an error in the data, so let's remove the two problematic cases. To do so we type

```
drop if grade < 4
```

Stata will report that it deleted two observations. Sometimes it is more efficient not to indicate which observations should be dropped, but which should be kept. Have a look at the variable occupation, which tells us in which job respondents work. Imagine that we want to have a dataset that only contains information about managers. We could use a drop command, with a condition that takes all other occupations and removes them. Using the complement and telling Stata which occupations to keep is much faster in this case, so try

```
keep if occupation == 2
```

Stata will tell you that it removed 1,982 observations. This command can be really helpful when you want to create new data files which only consist of subsets of your data, like an all male or female dataset.

Finally, we want to delete a variable that we do not need anymore. Note that in this case, the number of observations stays identical. We want to remove the ID variable that we created before, as we want to use the original variable ("idcode") instead. Try

```
drop ID
describe
```

variable name	storage type	display format	value label	variable label
idcode	int	%8.0g		NLS id
age	byte	%8.0g		age in current year
race	byte	%8.0g	racelbl	race
married	byte	%8.0g	marlbl	married
never_married	byte	%8.0g		never married
grade	byte	%8.0g		current grade completed
collgrad	byte	%16.0g	gradlbl	college graduate
south	byte	%8.0g		lives in south
smsa	byte	%9.0g	smsalbl	lives in SMSA
c_city	byte	%8.0g	yesno	lives in central city
industry	byte	%23.0g	indlbl	industry
occupation	byte	%22.0g	occlbl	occupation
union	byte	%8.0g	unionlbl	union worker
wage	float	%9.0g		hourly wage
hours	byte	%8.0g		usual hours worked
ttl_exp	float	%9.0g		total work experience
tenure	float	%9.0g		job tenure (years)
ind_ID	float	%9.0g		
ybirth	float	%9.0g		
tenure_cat	float	%9.0g		
maxvalue	float	%9.0g		
parttime	float	%9.0g		
is_white	byte	%9.0g	is_white	RECODE of race (race)

You will see that the variable is not listed anymore. Remember that *drop* combined with an if condition will remove cases, otherwise it will remove variables. If you actually executed the commands described here (*keep* and *drop*), make sure to reload your dataset before you proceed, otherwise you will receive different results (*sysuse nlsw88, clear*).

3.10 Cleaning data systematically

Someday you might work with large datasets that contain thousands of cases. Making sense of such amounts of information is not easy as individually reviewing and cleaning cases is not feasible anymore. Still chances are quite high that there are errors in the data. Even when you cannot correct the mistake, since the original or true information is missing, you can delete or flag these observations and not use them in your analyses.

One first thing you can do is check whether the values which are contained in your variables make sense. As an example, I want to use the variable age, which clearly has only a certain range of correct values. As only adults are interviewed, values below 18 should not be possible. Also there should be a limit since a value of 200 is quite impossible, yet can happen easily due to a typo. We will use the *assert* command to perform these "sanity checks" automatically

```
assert inrange(age,18,100)
```

Stata will halt if there is a contradiction found in the data, otherwise nothing will happen, which tells us that the assertion is fulfilled. The same goes for variables with ordinal scaling: as only a few values are defined (say from 1 to 5 on a rating scale), any other values are probably incorrect:

```
assert inrange(occupation,1,13)
```

This time you will receive an error, as the assertion is not fulfilled for all cases. Closer inspection shows that the problematic cases are ones with missing information. When you want to allow this to happen, you can adjust your assertion respectively

```
assert inrange(occupation,1,13) | missing(occupation)
```

Another common source of problems arises when several variables are linked in a logical way. For example, have a look at the two variables ttl_exp and tenure. The first measures the overall job experience of a woman, the second how long she works in her current job. Logically, the overall job experience must always be longer or equal to the time working for the current job, otherwise the information is contradictory and probably false. We can check it by typing

```
compare ttl_exp tenure
```

	count	minimum	difference average	maximum
ttl_exp=tenure	141			
ttl_exp>tenure	2090	.0064096	7.020712	21.47436
jointly defined	2231	0	6.577001	21.47436
tenure missing only	15			
total	2246			

Actually we see that ttl_exp is always larger or equal to tenure. A similar error can arise when questions depend on each other in a survey: when a person states that she is currently unemployed, but responds that she works 20 hours a week in the next question, there is something wrong. The same goes for children with a PhD or men with a hysterectomy. When you are new to surveys, you just would not believe how often data is just terribly incorrect when you receive it.

3.11 Combining datasets*

Sometimes you do not have one large dataset that contains all the information you need, but several files with different aspects. For example, one file could contain information about the personal characteristics of a respondent, like age or place of residence. Another file might contain information about the school career and grades. For analyses it is often necessary to bring these pieces of information together and combine datasets.

When you work with large professionally collected datasets, it is often the case that the creators of the data provide a rich set of information about how their datasets work, and how they can be combined. Still, it is required to think about which pieces of data you need to do your analyses. This is something you have to do in advance, which often involves switching between different datasets. I assume you know what you really want to do, and will show you five different cases you might encounter. Note that you can also apply all of the following procedures by using the interface. Just click **Data → Combine datasets** and choose the desired method.

3.11.1 Appending datasets

When you have several datasets that contain basically the same information, but about different observations, you can combine them all into one large dataset. For example, you have a questionnaire that you give to two colleagues. One goes to city A and interviews people, the other goes to city B. In the end, both bring you their datasets which contain the same variables, but for different persons (Table 3.2).

Table 3.2: Appending datasets (before).V

Dataset A			Dataset B		
Name	Age	Income	Name	Age	Income
Jeff	23	2300	John	18	1200
Dave	55	3400	Carol	66	1900

After appending you have one dataset that basically looks like this (Table 3.3):

Table 3.3: Appending datasets (after).

Name	Age	Income
Combined Dataset		
Jeff	23	2300
Dave	55	3400
John	18	1200
Carol	66	1900

To see this in action make sure that you saved your dataset that we used throughout this chapter, as we will create a new one now. First, open two datasets from the online database and save them locally on your computer:[6]

```
use "http://data.statabook.com/append_a_old.dta", clear
list
save "append_a", replace7
use "http://data.statabook.com/append_b.dta", clear
list
save "append_b", replace
```

We will append the saved file append_a.dta to the open dataset append_b.dta. In Stata we call the dataset that is open at the moment (in memory) the "Master" and the other one, that will be added, the "Using". Note that since version 11 you can also append several datasets at once.

```
append using "append_a", generate(check_append)
list
```

The *generate* option creates an indicator variable called check_append that later tells you which observation was added and which was from the original (in this case from "append_b"). With the *list* command, you can check whether everything went fine. Your new dataset should have six observations. When you want to use point-and-click go to **Data → Combine datasets → Append datasets.**

3.11.2 One-to-One Merge

The second case, that occurs more often in reality, is that you have several datasets from the same institute, and variables are separated by topic. To combine these

---

6 The files provided for the example work with Stata 15 or 14. If you are using an older version, you have to replace the file suffix with "_old.dta". For example, change append_a.dta to append_a_old.dta.
7 The option *replace* will overwrite any existing dataset with the same name, if existent.

datasets each of them has to include one unique identifier, like an ID, which is used to merge data correctly. Suppose the following basic design for the two files you want to merge (Table 3.4):

Table 3.4: 1:1 Merge (before).

Dataset A			Dataset B		
Country	Population	GDP	Country	Currency	Gini
USA	325	20.20	USA	US-Dollar	41.1
Germany	82	4.15	Germany	Euro	29.5
Japan	127	5.42	Japan	Yen	37.9

After merging these files you get (Table 3.5):

Table 3.5: 1:1 Merge (after).

Combined Dataset				
Country	Population	GDP	Currency	Gini
USA	325	20.20	US-Dollar	41.1
Germany	82	4.15	Euro	29.5
Japan	127	5.42	Yen	37.9

To make this work, both files that should be merged together must contain a unique identifier, in this case the name of the country. In interviews, this is often a unique number that is given to each participant and cannot occur twice *within* one dataset. When this variable does not exist and cannot be created, merging is not possible. Sometimes more than one variable is needed, for example, when the same people were interviewed over the course of some years, so the unique ID and the year would be needed. We will now try to do this by typing

```
use "http://data.statabook.com/1to1_a.dta", clear
list
save "1to1_a", replace
use "http://data.statabook.com/1to1_b.dta", clear
list
save "1to1_b", replace
merge 1:1 country using "1to1_a.dta"
list
```

Note that *country* is the unique identifier which contains the name of the country. Also take a look at the info Stata gives you after performing the merge. You will see that Stata created an indicator variable automatically this time (_merge). When you want to use point-and-click, go to **Data → Combine datasets → Merge two datasets**.

3.11.3 Many-to-One Merge

The third case will be used whenever there is asymmetry in the datasets. Maybe your main file contains information about pupils and which school they attend. You also have a second data file which contains information about the schools, like in which district they are placed and the number of pupils attending (Table 3.6). As there are many more pupils than schools, your school dataset has fewer observations than your main file. As long as there is a school ID in both datasets you can match the data.

Table 3.6: M:1 Merge (before).

Dataset A			Dataset B		
Name	Age	School ID	School ID	District	Size
Ken	15	101	101	North	2550
Anna	14	101	202	West	1230
Jack	16	202	303	South	1780
Sarah	12	303			
Dylan	14	303			

After merging these files you get (Table 3.7):

Table 3. 7: M:1 Merge (after).

Combined Dataset				
Name	Age	School ID	District	Size
Ken	15	101	North	2550
Anna	14	101	North	2550
Jack	16	202	West	1230
Sarah	12	303	South	1780
Dylan	14	303	South	1780

This merging is called many-to-one, as your master file (which is in memory at the time of merging) has more observations ("many") than your using file ("one"). Let's see this in action.

```
use "http://data.statabook.com/mto1_b.dta", clear
list
save "mto1_b", replace
use "http://data.statabook.com/mto1_a.dta", clear
list
save "mto1_a", replace
merge m:1 school_ID using "mto1_b.dta"
list
```

school_ID is the variable that links information about schools and pupils and, therefore, works as a unique identifier. Note that the file with the "many" (the pupils) has to be opened at the time of merging in memory.

3.11.4 One-to-Many Merge

Basically, this is exactly the same procedure as the Many-to-One Merge, but only the files for master and using are swapped. When you can perform a Many-to-One Merge you can always perform a One-to-Many Merge as well (and the other way round). To save space, you can just change the code above or look at the do-file provided for this chapter online.

3.11.5 All pairwise combinations

Imagine that you have two datasets, one about parents and one about their children (Table 3.8). As every child has two parents and some parents have more than one child, a direct match is not possible. When you have the child data as master, which parent would you link with the child, father or mother? The other way round, when you use the parent data as master and a family has several children, which of them would you merge to a parent? In these cases, you can form all pairwise combinations.

Table 3.8: All pairwise combinations (before).

Dataset A			Dataset B		
Family ID	Parent ID	Age (P)	Family ID	Child ID	Score (C)
A1	1	45	A1	1	127
A1	2	37	A2	1	101
A2	1	28	A2	2	99
A2	2	23	A2	3	109
A3	1	33	A3	1	131

After forming all pairwise combinations you get (Table 3.9):

Table 3.9: All pairwise combinations (after).

Combined Dataset				
Family ID	Parent ID	Age (P)	Child ID	Score (C)
A1	1	45	1	127
A1	2	37	1	127
A2	1	28	1	101

Table 3.9 (continued)

	Combined Dataset			
Family ID	Parent ID	Age (P)	Child ID	Score (C)
A2	1	28	2	99
A2	1	28	3	109
A2	2	23	1	101
A2	2	23	2	99
A2	2	23	3	109
A3	1	33	1	131

The number of all pairwise combinations is the product of the number of cases in each dataset with the same ID, thus two for family A1, six for family A2 and one for family A3. When one ID is only available in one of the two datasets, it will not be included in the resulting file (as any number times zero is zero. You can change that standard option if you want). Now for the example:

```
use "http://data.statabook.com/pairs_a.dta", clear
list
save "pairs_a", replace
use "http://data.statabook.com/pairs_b.dta", clear
list
save "pairs_b", replace
joinby family_ID using "pairs_a"        //Form pairs
sort family_ID child_ID                 //Sort data
list, sepby(family_ID)                  //List results
```

Merging datasets can be confusing for beginners, yet can be mastered with time and practice. The key to correct merging is reading the documentation of your datasets (sorry, no magic trick here!) and learning how they are structured (use *describe*, *list* and *browse*). If you read this chapter twice, and still think none of the solutions described here is the correct one for you, it could be the case that you cannot merge your data. When you can't find a unique identifier (or more than one) that links cases throughout files, a merge will end in chaos. Do not try the Many-to-Many Merge as even the Stata documentation itself advises against ever using it!

3.12 Reshaping data*

Someday you might want to work with panel- or history-data. In these cases the same people are interviewed several times, say, once every year. Or maybe you have information about the development of countries and want to see the trends over time. In these cases, it is often necessary to reshape data. What sounds complex is quite simple in Stata. Basically you only have two options, the wide format (Table 3.10) and the long format (Table 3.11). The wide format is used when every case (observation, person, country, etc...) needs exactly one line in the data browser to show all of its information. Cross-sectional designs are in almost all cases in the wide format, and reshaping is not needed here. When you have time-series-data (e.g. panel-data), they can have both shapes, and we want to show how to transform this kind of data.

Table 3.10: Data in wide format.

Wide Format				
Country	Currency	Score2010	Score2011	Score2012
USA	US-Dollar	1000	1010	1015
Germany	Euro	930	980	990
Japan	Yen	1200	1120	1150

This dataset contains some kind of ID (the name of the country), a variable, that does not change over time (the currency), a score that does change over time, and the values for each year are saved as an extra variable. We want to reshape to long format, where one country can take several lines and we will introduce a new year-variable. The reshaped format would look like this:

Table 3.11: Data in long format.

Long Format			
Country	Year	Currency	Score
USA	2010	US-Dollar	1000
USA	2011	US-Dollar	1010
USA	2012	US-Dollar	1015
Germany	2010	Euro	930
Germany	2011	Euro	980
Germany	2012	Euro	990
Japan	2010	Yen	1200
Japan	2011	Yen	1120
Japan	2012	Yen	1150

A new variable that indicates the point in time (year) was created, and some variables were deleted, as they are no longer needed. Time constant variables are the same in every year, as they do not change. To reshape data, you need two pieces of information: an ID, that identifies every object in your data (in our example, the country) and the point in time (in our example years, which is an extra variable in the long format and merged into the name of another variable in the wide format). As always, to perform a successful reshape, it is vital to be familiar with the dataset used. We have an example where we reshape wide to long, and then back to wide:

```
use "http://data.statabook.com/reshape.dta", clear
list
reshape long score@, i(country) j(year)        //Wide to long
list, sepby(country)
```

If you prefer point-and-click, go **Data → Create or change data → Other variable-transformation commands → Convert data between wide and long**.

We first open the dataset and inspect it. We notice that each country has exactly one line, so we know it is wide. We identify the variable that changes (score) and see that it contains a fixed part (the front part) and a changing part (the suffix). This is why we use the @-sign to tell Stata which part is changing (note that this is optional). Then we identify the ID (country) and think of a name for the newly created variable (year), which does not exist yet.

To go back, we use exactly the same command and only change the desired format:

```
reshape wide score@, i(country) j(year)        //Long to wide
list
```

As long as you do not create any time-varying variables additionally, you can also use the shorter commands to switch between the formats, after having used the explicit commands before:

```
reshape long                        //Go to long format
reshape wide                        //Go to wide format
```

4 Describing data

After you have cleaned your data, checked for errors and problems and created new variables, it is time to describe your data. Every piece of scientific research, no matter whether it is a seminar paper or a thesis, will include a part where you just describe what you see. No fancy causal analyses or advanced statistical methods are needed here, just reporting means, medians, tables or the distribution of variables, so the reader can get an impression what the data is all about. Furthermore, descriptive parts are also extremely relevant for yourself as a good description always helps in understanding the phenomena you want to explore. In this chapter you will learn how to do this.

The Fre command

In the last chapter you have already encountered the *tabulate* command, which is used to inspect variables or create crosstabs. While the command is really good for the second task, when it comes to just looking at one variable, there is a better option available. This is the *fre* command (Jann, 2007) which creates clear and concise information about variables, and offers many useful options. The biggest advantage, in comparison to the standard tabulate command, is the fact that *fre* always displays numerical values next to the value labels, which is a real boon for recoding. To install, just type

```
ssc install fre, replace
fre industry
```

industry — industry

			Freq.	Percent	Valid	Cum.
Valid	1	Ag/Forestry/Fisheries	17	0.76	0.76	0.76
	2	Mining	4	0.18	0.18	0.94
	3	Construction	29	1.29	1.30	2.24
	4	Manufacturing	367	16.34	16.44	18.68
	5	Transport/Comm/Utility	90	4.01	4.03	22.72
	6	Wholesale/Retail Trade	333	14.83	14.92	37.63
	7	Finance/Ins/Real Estate	192	8.55	8.60	46.24
	8	Business/Repair Svc	86	3.83	3.85	50.09
	9	Personal Services	97	4.32	4.35	54.44
	10	Entertainment/Rec Svc	17	0.76	0.76	55.20
	11	Professional Services	824	36.69	36.92	92.11
	12	Public Administration	176	7.84	7.89	100.00
		Total	2232	99.38	100.00	
Missing	.		14	0.62		
Total			2246	100.00		

It will be downloaded automatically from the web database, as it is community-contributed software. Throughout the book we will use the *tabulate* command, as this is the standard, and always available. Yet, I encourage you to compare both commands and see what helps you most in dealing with your own projects.

When you cannot use *fre*, but still want more comfort with the classical *tabulate* command, try the following after loading your dataset

https://doi.org/10.1515/9783110617160-004

```
numlabel, add
tabulate industry
```

industry	Freq.	Percent	Cum.
1. Ag/Forestry/Fisheries	17	0.76	0.76
2. Mining	4	0.18	0.94
3. Construction	29	1.30	2.24
4. Manufacturing	367	16.44	18.68
5. Transport/Comm/Utility	90	4.03	22.72
6. Wholesale/Retail Trade	333	14.92	37.63
7. Finance/Ins/Real Estate	192	8.60	46.24
8. Business/Repair Svc	86	3.85	50.09
9. Personal Services	97	4.35	54.44
10. Entertainment/Rec Svc	17	0.76	55.20
11. Professional Services	824	36.92	92.11
12. Public Administration	176	7.89	100.00
Total	2,232	100.00	

Stata automatically added numerical labels to all categories. This is quite convenient, yet has the drawback that missing cases are still not shown automatically. Furthermore, the labels will be only added to existing variables, so you have to run the command again after you created new variables. Lastly, the labels added will also show up in the graphics you produce, which can be annoying. To get rid of the labels again type

```
numlabel, remove
```

4.1 Summarizing information

By now we have used the *tabulate* command several times to get an impression of our data, but as variables can contain thousands of different numerical values, this is not a good way to summarize information. This is usually done by employing statistical indicators such as the mean, median or standard deviation. Stata can compute these numbers easily, which of course requires a variable with an inherent metric (remember that you should not summarize nominal or ordinal variables in this fashion, as the results can be meaningless). We will use the same dataset as in the last chapter. A great variable to test this is age, so let's see this in action

```
sysuse nlsw88, clear          //Open dataset
summarize age, detail
```

or click **Statistics → Summaries, tables, and tests → Summary and descriptive statistics → Summary statistics.** You will receive a table indicating the (arithmetic) mean (39.15), the standard deviation (3.06) and the number of cases used (2,246).

```
                     age in current year

         Percentiles       Smallest
   1%         34               34
   5%         35               34
  10%         35               34         Obs              2,246
  25%         36               34         Sum of Wgt.      2,246

  50%         39                          Mean          39.15316
                           Largest        Std. Dev.     3.060002
  75%         42               45
  90%         44               45         Variance      9.363614
  95%         44               46         Skewness      .2003234
  99%         45               46         Kurtosis      1.932389
```

When some persons have missing values for a variable, you would notice it here. The left part of the table computes certain values as percentiles. Remember that the median is the 50% percentile. In our case that means that 50% of all persons are 39 years old or younger, while 50% are older than 39. When you need a percentile that is not listed here, like 33%, try the *centile* command:

```
centile age, centile(33)
```

```
                                                   — Binom. Interp. —
   Variable  |   Obs   Percentile   Centile    [95% Conf. Interval]

        age  |  2,246       33         37           37          37
```

or click **Statistics → Summaries, tables, and tests → Summary and descriptive statistics → Centiles with Cis**. The result is 37, meaning that one third of the sample are younger or equal to 37 years old, while two thirds are older than that age. If you want to learn more about the other statistics presented, refer to your statistics textbook.

In a seminar paper, you should report the most basic statistics for relevant dependent and independent variables, like the mean, standard deviation, median and number of observations. Doing this is quite easy and can be done using all variables at the same time, as long as you only include metric, binary or ordinal numbers:

```
summarize age never_married collgrad union wage
```

```
      Variable  |    Obs       Mean     Std. Dev.      Min        Max

           age  |  2,246   39.15316    3.060002        34         46
   never_marr~d |  2,246   .1041852    .3055687         0          1
      collgrad  |  2,246   .2368655    .4252538         0          1
         union  |  1,878   .2454739    .4304825         0          1
          wage  |  2,246   7.766949    5.755523   1.004952   40.74659
```

As long as your binary variables are coded in a 0/1 fashion, you can include them as well, as the mean is just the percentage with a value of 1. To export such a table into your text-editor, you can highlight the table in Stata, right-click and copy it directly.

Unfortunately, this will often not yield the desired results. To get nicer results, you can use a user-written script (CCS).

```
ssc install estout, replace                          //install CCS
estpost summarize age never_married collgrad union wage
esttab using "out.rtf", cells("mean sd min max") noobs
```

Figure 4.1: Exporting tables.

The last command creates a nicely formatted table, in a new .rtf-document, in your current working directory (Figure 4.1). The options in parentheses, after cells, specify which statistics to include. Using this script makes it quite convenient to export tables and use them directly in your publications, with only little adjustments needed afterwards. Make sure to read the official documentation for the command, as it is very powerful and offers many options.[1]

4.2 Using stored results*

Sometimes you calculate statistics, to further use them in an algorithm or to transform data. For example, you can use the mean and the standard deviation to z-standardize[2] a metric variable. By doing so, the transformed variable will have a mean of zero and a standard deviation of one, which is often helpful in regressions. Normally, you would tell Stata to calculate the mean and the standard deviation, write down the values and plug them into a formula to generate the new variable, for example

---

1 http://repec.sowi.unibe.ch/stata/estout/ (2018-05-16).

2 $Score_z = \dfrac{x_i - \bar{x}}{SD\,(x)}$

```
summarize wage, detail
```
– output omitted –

You see that the mean is 7.77 and the standard deviation is 5.76. Now you generate the new variable

```
generate z_wage = (wage-7.77)/5.76
```

Luckily this can be done faster, as many Stata commands not only display the numbers but also store them internally for other uses. To see what Stata stores, run the command (*summarize*) again (as only the results of the last command will be stored) and try

```
return list³
```
scalars:
```
            r(N)  =   2246
        r(sum_w)  =   2246
         r(mean)  =   7.76694903741006
          r(Var)  =   33.12604338487759
           r(sd)  =   5.755522859382768
     r(skewness)  =   3.096199110442575
     r(kurtosis)  =   15.85446401424329
          r(sum)  =   17444.567538023
          r(min)  =   1.00495183467865
          r(max)  =   40.74658966064453
           r(p1)  =   1.930992722511292
           r(p5)  =   2.801002025604248
          r(p10)  =   3.220612049102783
          r(p25)  =   4.259257316589356
          r(p50)  =   6.272270202636719
          r(p75)  =   9.597423553466797
          r(p90)  =   12.77777481079102
          r(p95)  =   16.52978897094727
          r(p99)  =   38.70925903320313
```

You will see a list of all statistics Stata saves. You can use them directly

```
quietly summarize wage, detail⁴              //Do not show output
generate z_wage2 = (wage-r(mean))/r(sd)
summarize z_wage2                            //Check result
```

Variable	Obs	Mean	Std. Dev.	Min	Max
z_wage2	2,246	-5.09e-10	1	-1.174871	5.730086

We see that the overall mean is very close to zero. The difference is only due to rounding.

---

3 Some commands, like *regress*, use the command *ereturn list* as they *estimated* a model.
4 Whenever you put *quietly* in front of a command, Stata will not show the output but still keeps the calculated results in memory, which is a useful trick.

4.3 Histograms

While central statistics, as discussed above, are important, sometimes you want to show the actual distribution of a variable. Histograms are a good way to do this for metric variables. Try

histogram age

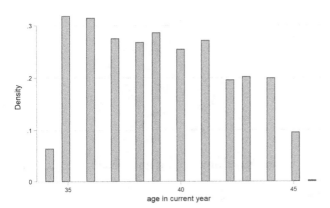

or click **Graphics → Histograms**. When you are used to working with histograms, the result might disappoint you as white areas between the bars are not common for this kind graphic. The problem here is that, although the variable has an inherent metric, due to the special sample, there are only a few distinct values (from 34 to 46). To get a nicer graph type

histogram age, discrete

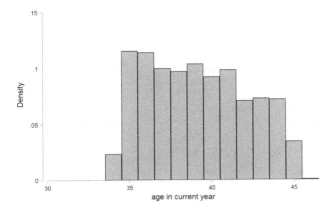

or choose the option *Data are discrete* from the menu.

Another type of graphic, that is related to histograms, are kernel-density plots that offer a smoother view of the distribution:

```
kdensity age
```

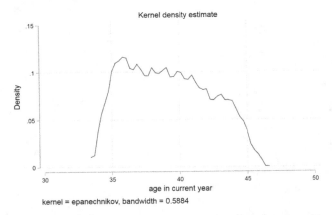

You will find this graphic under **Graphics → Smoothing and densities → Kernel density estimation.**

When you want to combine several plots within one graph, you can use the command *twoway*:

```
twoway (kdensity wage if collgrad==0) (kdensity wage if collgrad==1)
```

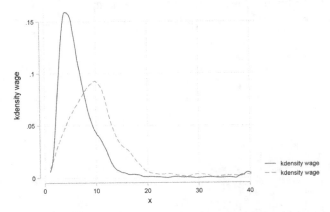

or click **Graphics → Twoway graph** and create the subgraphs separately. Note that, although the command is called *twoway*, you can combine an arbitrary number of plots in one graph. The code for each subplot has to be enclosed in parentheses.

4.4 Boxplots

Another way to create clear and concise graphics for metric variables is via boxplots. Try it by typing

```
graph box wage
```

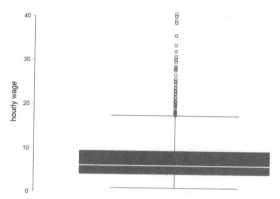

or click **Graphics → Box plot**.

You see one box with a thick line in it which marks the median (the second quartile). The lower bound of the box is the first quartile, the upper bound is the third quartile. Therefore, the box includes 50% of all observations around the median, and the distance from lower to upper bound is also called the interquartile range. The other two limits, which are connected to the box, are the whiskers of the boxplot. The distance from the box to the end of the whisker is at most 1.5 times the size of the interquartile range. All observations that are outside the whiskers are outliers (per definition) and depicted by dots. Note that the length of the whiskers can be smaller if there are no observations beyond. Thus, in our case, the lower whisker is shorter than the upper (as the smallest value is 1.0).

Boxplots are also very practical for comparing metric values between groups. Try

```
graph box wage, over(union)
```

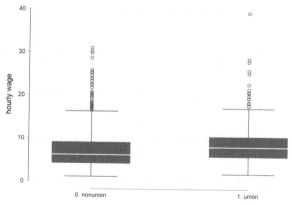

Dealing with outliers

Using histograms or the *sum* command provides a great opportunity to inspect variables quickly. By doing this, you will notice that outliers are a common problem. Outliers are cases that have extremely small, or large, numerical values on metric variables that are rather uncommon. For example, let's inspect the variable wage visually, by typing

```
histogram wage
```

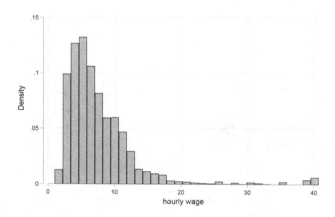

You will notice that there is a large proportion of the values between 0 and 15, while there are only very few cases beyond that. What you consider an outlier depends on your research question, your data and your personal opinion, as there is no general rule to classify them. Basically you have three options to continue:
1. **Do nothing.** Just leave the variable unchanged and work with it. This can work very well, but sometimes outliers can influence your regression results significantly. You should probably invest some time, and try to find out why there are outliers, as there might be a coding problem or error in the data. If this is not true, and the data is correct, you should have a closer look at the respective cases as there might be an interesting hidden subpopulation for further research.
2. **Fix them.** You can fix outliers to a numerical limit, say 25. So every value that is larger than 25 will be set to this value. You can do this by typing

```
replace wage = 25 if wage > 25 & !missing(wage)
```

    Pay attention to the part !missing(wage) as otherwise all people with missing values on this variable will also receive this value, which would be a severe mistake. The general problem with this technique is that it reduces the variance of your variable, as the values above the limit, which can be different from each other, will all be set to the same value.
3. **Remove them.** Sometimes you can exclude any cases from your analysis that are outliers. This means you will not use these observations. Say again, that our limit is 25, so we type

```
replace wage = . if wage > 25
```

All cases with larger values will be set to a missing value, and thus not used. This option can introduce bias, as in this case, you remove some special groups from your analyses; namely people with high incomes.

You have to think theoretically, when certain subgroups are not included in your study, as to what this can do to your research question.

Whatever you do, make sure to write about it in your research paper, so the reader knows how you processed the data. And make sure to reload the original dataset if you executed the commands described here, otherwise your results will differ from the ones presented here.

4.5 Simple bar charts

Let's have a look at the variable industry, which tells us the branches respondents work in. We type

```
tabulate industry
```

industry	Freq.	Percent	Cum.
Ag/Forestry/Fisheries	17	0.76	0.76
Mining	4	0.18	0.94
Construction	29	1.30	2.24
Manufacturing	367	16.44	18.68
Transport/Comm/Utility	90	4.03	22.72
Wholesale/Retail Trade	333	14.92	37.63
Finance/Ins/Real Estate	192	8.60	46.24
Business/Repair Svc	86	3.85	50.09
Personal Services	97	4.35	54.44
Entertainment/Rec Svc	17	0.76	55.20
Professional Services	824	36.92	92.11
Public Administration	176	7.89	100.00
Total	2,232	100.00	

and receive a table that lists frequencies. Let's suppose we want to convert this information into a bar chart, so it can be represented visually, and that we want to plot the absolute number of frequencies for each category. Oddly, there is no easy way to do directly this in Stata. One possibility is to use the *histogram* command with a lot of options, that somehow brings us closer to what we want, but it is complicated and often not exceptionally pretty. Especially, when a variable has many categories and you want to label them all, it gets tricky. Luckily, someone before us noticed this problem and wrote a little command (community-contributed software) that helps us out. Type

```
ssc install catplot, replace        //install CCS
catplot industry, blabel(bar)       //plot variable
```

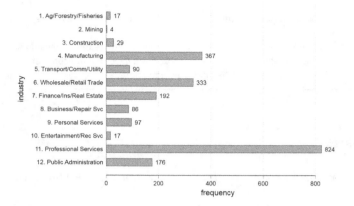

I hope this is roughly what you want. Note that you can customize the command by using options from the *graph bar* command. When you do not want to show the absolute numbers for each category, just remove the option *blabel(bar)*. In general, Stata offers a variety of different graphs, and many sophisticated options to customize them. While this is a boon to the experienced user, beginners are often deterred from using the many possibilities. It is a good way to start with simple graphs, and use the point-and-click menu to try out different options to see what they do. Over time, you will build a personal preference for certain forms of representing data visually, and you will be able to create them easily. Make sure to always save your commands in a do-file, so you can look them up quickly later. When it comes to documenting how graphs are created, Stata is clearly outstanding.

4.6 Scatterplots

Whenever you want a visual representation of the relation of two metric variables, scatterplots are a good idea. They are used to check whether two variables are somehow related to each other, and whether there is any hint of a correlation visible. To see this in action, we want to plot the relation of wages to total work experience. We assume that people with more experience will earn more on average. We type

```
scatter wage ttl_exp
```

or click **Graphics → Twoway graph (scatter, line, etc.)** and click **Create...** and enter the x- and y-variable. The first variable (wage) goes on the y-axis, the second one (ttl_exp) on the x-axis. We can see that there seems to be some relation, yet as we have many data points, due to the high number of observations, some kind of thick cloud is created at the bottom making a visual inspection difficult. To account for this, we can try the option *jitter*

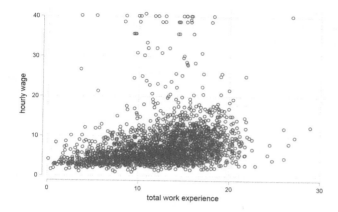

```
scatter wage ttl_exp, jitter(10)
```
– output omitted –

This is also extremely helpful when dealing with variables which do not have many distinct values. Basically, it creates a standard scatterplot and moves every data point slightly, and in a random fashion to the side so points are not plotted exactly on top of each other. The numerical value (in our case 10) is a value that tells Stata how strong this random movement should be. Another solution is to use the *color* option:

```
scatter wage ttl_exp, color(%20)
```

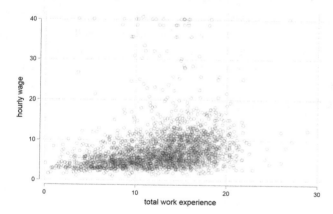

The number in parentheses can be between 1 and 100, and lets you adjust the saturation of the dots. When you want to get an even clearer visualization, try the CCS *binscatter*[5] (you need Stata 13 or newer to use this). This command combines data

---

5 https://michaelstepner.com/binscatter/ (2018-01-29).

points and, therefore, reduces their number but still recovers the overall tendency of the distribution, and also fits a linear model.

```
ssc install binscatter, replace              //install CCS
binscatter wage ttl_exp
```

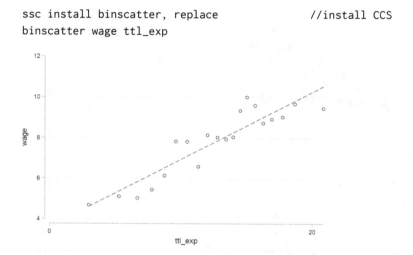

4.7 Frequency tables

Simple tables are at the heart of science, as they can summarize a great load of information in a few lines. While fancy graphics might be useful in presentations, scientific publications should mostly rely on tables, even when they seem plain or boring. Stata offers a great variety of options for creating customized tables which we will explore in detail. We already know how to inspect the distribution of values, for one variable, using the *tabulate* command, and how to create crosstabs (see page 33). We want to expand these tables, to gain further insight, and analyze how the variables, union and south, are related, to check whether there are differences between the regions (south vs not south).

```
tabulate union south
```

union worker	lives in south 0	1	Total
nonunion	754	663	1,417
union	325	136	461
Total	1,079	799	1,878

Alternatively, click **Statistics → Summaries, tables, and tests → Frequency tables → Two-way table with measures of association.**

This yields a simple crosstab with plain frequencies. Often, not absolute numbers but percentages are more interesting, when searching effects. First, note that the variable union

defines the rows of your table, and the variable south, the columns. We could summarize by column:

tabulate union south, column

Key
frequency
column percentage

union worker	lives in south		
	0	1	Total
nonunion	754	663	1,417
	69.88	82.98	75.45
union	325	136	461
	30.12	17.02	24.55
Total	1,079	799	1,878
	100.00	100.00	100.00

Stata then displays percentages. We can compare relative interests in unions by region.
In the south, only 17% are union members, while in other regions, this number is
over 30%. We can deduct from this, that unions are much more popular in non-south
regions than in the south (assuming that our data is representative of women from
the USA). Or to formulate it differently: imagine you are in the south and talk to a randomly chosen woman. The chances that she is a union member would be about 17%.
    We can also summarize differently by typing

tabulate union south, row

Key
frequency
row percentage

union worker	lives in south		
	0	1	Total
nonunion	754	663	1,417
	53.21	46.79	100.00
union	325	136	461
	70.50	29.50	100.00
Total	1,079	799	1,878
	57.45	42.55	100.00

Stata summarizes, this time by row. Here we have to think in a different manner. Let's
suppose you visit a large convention of union members who are representative of the
USA. When you talk to a random union member, the chance that she is from the south is

29.5%. Please take some time to think about the major differences when you summarize by row or column. What you choose must be theoretically justified for your individual research question.

A third option is to show the relative frequency of each cell:

tabulate union south, cell

Key
frequency
cell percentage

union worker	lives in south		
	0	1	Total
nonunion	754	663	1,417
	40.15	35.30	75.45
union	325	136	461
	17.31	7.24	24.55
Total	1,079	799	1,878
	57.45	42.55	100.00

This enables you to say that in your sample 40.15% of all respondents are not union members and are not from the south. Theoretically, you can also combine all options in one large table:

tabulate union south, column row cell

Key
frequency
row percentage
column percentage
cell percentage

union worker	lives in south		
	0	1	Total
nonunion	754	663	1,417
	53.21	46.79	100.00
	69.88	82.98	75.45
	40.15	35.30	75.45
union	325	136	461
	70.50	29.50	100.00
	30.12	17.02	24.55
	17.31	7.24	24.55
Total	1,079	799	1,878
	57.45	42.55	100.00
	100.00	100.00	100.00
	57.45	42.55	100.00

This is usually not a good idea as this table is very hard to read, and can easily lead to errors. Often it is a better idea to use more tables, than to create a super table with all possible options.

Another less common option I want to discuss here is 3-way-tables. Until now, we have looked at two variables at once, but we can do better. By introducing a third variable we can get even further insight. Imagine we want to assess the influence of the size of the city the respondent lives in. We have a binary variable as we count some cities as central and others not. To test the influence, we type

```
table union south, by(c_city)
```

lives in central city and union worker	lives in south	
	0	1
0		
nonunion	570	464
union	218	70
1		
nonunion	184	199
union	107	66

You can create this table by clicking **Statistics → Summaries, tables and tests → Other tables → Flexible table of summary statistics**. There you enter c_city under *Superrow variables*, union under *Row variable,* and south under *Column variable.* Then click **Submit**. Another possibility is to use the *bysort* command to create these kinds of tables (for example: *bysort c_city: tabulate union south*).

Note that these 3-way-tables are difficult to read and nowadays there are better ways to analyze your data. In the past, when computational power was much lower, these kinds of tables were at the heart of social sciences. You will find them in many older publications.

4.8 Summarizing information by categories

When you have a categorical variable, which is relevant to your research question, it is often a good idea to compare across categories. For example, we could check whether completing college has any effect on your later income. We can use the binary variable collgrad, which tells us whether a respondent finished college. We can summarize the wage by typing

```
tabulate collgrad, summarize(wage)
```

```
Summary for variables: wage
     by categories of: collgrad (college graduate)
```

collgrad	mean	sd	p50
not college grad	6.910561	5.283132	5.636071
college grad	10.52606	6.325833	9.677936
Total	7.766949	5.755523	6.27227

or click **Statistics → Summaries, tables, and tests → Other tables → Compact table of summary statistics.** Under *Variable 1*, enter collgrad and under *Summarize variable* wage, then click **Submit**. We notice a stark contrast between the means (6.9 VS 10.5) which tells us that, on average, people who finish college earn more.

When you want you can also combine frequency tables and summary statistics and produce detailed information for subgroups. Try

```
tabulate union south, summarize(wage)
```

```
        Means, Standard Deviations and Frequencies of hourly wage
```

union worker	lives in south 0	1	Total
nonunion	7.8266582	6.4973084	7.2046688
	4.2736995	3.7820647	4.1036938
	754	663	1417
union	8.9737177	7.9587599	8.6742941
	3.9529789	4.5984783	4.1745389
	325	136	461
Total	8.172158	6.7460661	7.5654235
	4.2109087	3.9680742	4.1683693
	1079	799	1878

You will receive information about the mean, standard deviation and the absolute frequency, separately for each cell of the table.

When you generally prefer graphs over simple tables, we can easily create a bar chart by typing

```
graph bar (mean) wage, over(collgrad) blabel(bar)
```

or clicking **Graphics → Bar chart**, tick the first line, enter *Mean* in the first field and wage in the second. Then click **Categories**, tick *Group 1* and enter collgrad. Then click **Bars** and tick *Label with bar height*. You can produce more complex graphs by introducing more categorical variables, e.g. south:

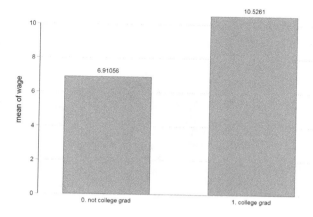

```
graph bar (mean) wage, over(collgrad) over(south) blabel(bar)
```

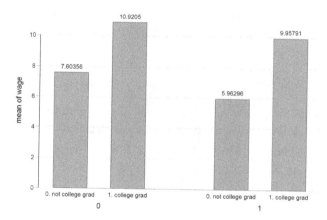

Note that these graphs get more and more complex, so be careful that the readability is not lost in the process. If you are not happy with the format of the numbers displayed, you can change this. For example, replace *blabel(bar)* with *blabel(bar, format(%5.2f))*. The 5 is the total number of digits displayed and the 2 specifies how many digits should appear after the decimal point. f specifies that the fixed format will be used (alternatives include exponential formats, and many more). Formatting is a quite complex, yet not so popular issue, so I refer you to the help files (type *help format*). Just remember that the format option displayed here works with many more graphs and tables and will be enough to create nicely formatted graphics easily.

Another option for comparing groups are dot charts. For example, when you want to compare mean wages in different occupations, try

```
graph dot (mean) wage, over(occupation)
```

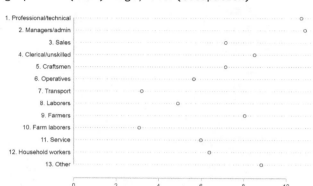

or click **Graphics → Dot chart**. By comparing both commands, you will notice that the syntax is almost identical, as only the *bar* is switched to *dot*. When you work with Stata for some time, you will get a feeling for the basic structure of commands, which are often similar.

4.9 Editing and exporting graphs

Producing graphics using commands, or point-and-click, is quite easy in Stata. This last part about graphs will show you how to finalize and export pretty graphs that could be used for publishing. To begin with an example, we will produce a simple histogram as before

```
histogram age, discrete
```

– output omitted –

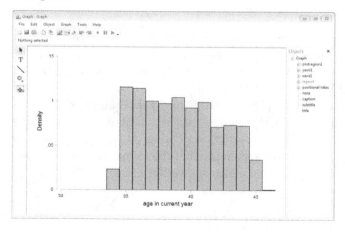

Figure 4.2: Stata's Graph Editor.

A new window will open which shows the graph (Figure 4.2). This is fine, but we will add a caption and our sources. In the new window click **File → Start Graph Editor**.

Another window will open that shows some additional elements. You can now either click the element you want to edit in the graph directly, or click the elements on the right-hand side of the screen. This part of the window lists, in detail, all elements that make up the graph. We could now start to edit these, but we want to record the changes we make. This can be pretty useful, for example, when you want to export several graphs and add the same details to all of them. Then you only need to record your scheme once, and later apply it to all graphs. To do this click **Tools → Recorder → Begin**. Now we start editing by clicking "note" and enter "Source: NLSW88" and click **Submit**. Then we click **Tool → Recorder → End** to finish our recording and give a name for the scheme (nlsw88).[6] To later use recorded schemes, we open the desired graph, start the Graph Editor and click **Tool → Recorder → Play** and choose the desired recording. As we want to keep it that simple, we click **File → Save as...** and save the file as histogram_age.gph. This is Stata's own file format and can only be used in Stata. Then we click **File → Stop Graph Editor**, which closes the Editor window. We can now export the graph, so we can use it in a text editor. We click **File → Save as...** and save it as "histogram_age.png". Preferred file formats are **.png** (which is a good idea when you want to use the graph in text editors or on websites) or as **.pdf**[7] (which makes upscaling for posters convenient). The corresponding commands are

```
histogram age, discrete                              //Create
graph save "histogram_age.gph", replace              //Save
graph export "histogram_age.png", as(png) replace    //Export
```

It is usually a good idea to save a graph first in Stata's own format (.gph). When you notice a mistake later, or want to make a change, this is impossible with an exported file and you have to start from the beginning. Gph-Files make it easy to edit already created graphs, and export them again to any desired format.

4.9.1 Combining graphs

Sometimes you want to show several graphs in a paper to give the reader an overview of the data. You can either produce one graph for each variable or combine several graphs. This is often preferred when it comes to descriptive statistics as space is usually short and compressing information, especially when it is not the most

---

6 Recordings are not saved in the current working directory. On Windows they are found in "C:\ado\personal\grec", on Linux in "/home/username/ado/personal/grec" and on Mac in "home/username/Library/Application Support/Stata/ado/personal/grec"
7 An alternative are svg-files, which were introduced in version 15.

interesting one, is a good idea. The basic idea here is to create each graph separately, give it a name, and later combine them.

First we start by creating the graphs:

```
histogram age, discrete name(age)
histogram wage, name(wage)
```

Each command produces a graph and labels it with a name (internally). Even when you now close the graph window, without saving it to your drive, it is still kept in memory as it has been named. When you want to change an already existing graph use the *replace* option

```
histogram age, title(Age) discrete name(age, replace)
```

Now we combine the two graphs into one image and label it as well:

```
graph combine age wage, name(age_wage)
```

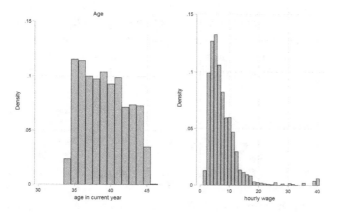

You can start the Graph Editor, and make changes to each graph individually as all information is saved in the process. Naming graphs is also possible when you use point-and-click. You can find the respective option under the category "Overall". When you do not name your graphs, the one you created last will be named "Graph" automatically. Note that only the one created most recently will be kept in memory, all other unnamed ones will be lost.

To conclude this very short introduction to graphs, I encourage you to explore the vast possibilities Stata offers when editing graphs, as they cannot be explained here. Actually, there is an entire book about creating and editing graphs in Stata (Mitchell, 2012). Shorter overviews can be found in the provided do-files for this chapter and online[8]

---

8 https://www.ssc.wisc.edu/sscc/pubs/4-24.htm (2018-02-21) or http://data.princeton.edu/stata/graphics.html (2018-02-21).

4.10 Correlations

As you have seen by now, it is quite easy to create helpful graphics out of your data. Sometimes it is a good idea to start with a visual aid, in order to get an idea of how the data is distributed, and switch to a numerical approach that can be reported easily in the text, and helps to pinpoint the strength of their effects. A classical approach is to use correlation, which measures how two variables covary with each other. For example, if we assume that the correlation between wage and total job experience is positive, more job experience will be associated with a higher wage. Basically, you have a positive correlation when one numerical value increases, and the other increases as well. Meanwhile, a negative correlation means that when you increase the value of one variable, the other one will decrease.

We can calculate this formally by typing

```
pwcorr wage ttl_exp, sig
```

	wage	ttl_exp
wage	1.0000	
ttl_exp	0.2655	1.0000
	0.0000	

or click **Statistics → Summaries, tables, and tests → Summary and descriptive statistics → Pairwise correlations**. Personally, I prefer the pairwise correlations command (*pwcorr*), as it additionally displays significance levels, whereas, the standard command (*correlate*) does not. The result tells us that the association is positive, with a value of 0.266 in the medium range.[9] How you assess the strength of a correlation depends mostly on your field of study. In finance this value might be viewed as extremely weak, while in the social sciences this seems like an interesting result that requires further investigation. Note that this command calculates Pearson's R, which is used for two metric variables. Stata also calculates correlations for other scales, like Spearman's Rho or Kendall's Rank correlation coefficient (both require at least two ordinally scaled variables), so try

```
spearman wage grade                //Spearman's Rho
   Number of obs =     2244
Spearman's rho =        0.4523

Test of Ho: wage and grade are independent
     Prob > |t| =        0.0000
```

---

9 Remember that a correlation is in the range from –1 (perfect negative association) to +1 (perfect positive association). A value of zero indicates that there is no linear relation at all (while there still can be a nonlinear one, so make sure to check this using scatterplots).

or click **Statistics → Nonparametric analysis → Tests of hypotheses → Spearman's rank correlation**.

Stata not only calculates Spearman's Rho (0.45), but also tests whether the association between the two variables specified is statistically significant. As the displayed result is smaller than 0.05, we know that this is the case. The conclusion is that the correlation coefficient is significantly different from zero.

```
ktau wage grade                 //Kendall's Tau

  Number of obs =     2244
Kendall's tau-a =       0.2987
Kendall's tau-b =       0.3379
Kendall's score =   751825
    SE of score =    34043.277   (corrected for ties)

Test of Ho: wage and grade are independent
    Prob > |z| =       0.0000  (continuity corrected)
```

If you want to use point-and-click, go **Statistics → Nonparametric analysis → Tests of hypotheses → Kendall's rank correlation**.

For more information on the different taus consult your statistics textbook. Also bear in mind that the *ktau* command is compute-intensive, and will take more time with larger datasets.

4.11 Testing for normality

Sometimes you want to know whether the distribution of a metric variable follows the normal distribution. To test this you have several options. The first is to use histograms to visually inspect how close the distribution of your variable of interest resembles a normal distribution (see page 51). By adding the option *normal* Stata furthermore includes the normal distribution plot to ease comparison.

If this seems a little crude, you can use quantile-quantile plots (Q-Q plots). This graphic plots expected against empirical data points. Just type

```
qnorm ttl_exp
```

or click **Statistics → Summaries, tables, and tests → Distributional plots and tests → Normal quantile plot**. The further the plotted points deviate from the straight line, the less the distribution of your variable follows a normal distribution.

If you prefer statistical tests, you can use the Shapiro-Wilk test (*swilk*, up to 2,000 cases), the Shapiro-Francia test (*sfrancia*, up to 5,000 cases) or the Skewness/Kurtosis test (*sktest*, for even more cases). As we have about 2,200 cases in our data, we will use the Shapiro-Francia test:

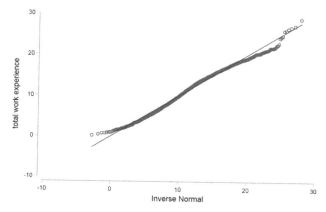

```
sfrancia ttl_exp
```

```
        Shapiro-Francia W' test for normal data
```

Variable	Obs	W'	V'	z	Prob>z
ttl_exp	2,246	0.98778	17.065	6.842	0.00001

or click **Statistics → Summaries, tables, and tests → Distributional plots and tests → Shapiro-Francia normality test**.

The test result is significant (Prob>z is smaller than 0.05). Therefore, we reject the null-hypothesis (which assumes a normal distribution for your variable) and come to the conclusion that the variable is not normally distributed. Keep in mind that these numerical tests are quite strict, and even small deviations will lead to a rejection of the assumption of normality.

4.12 t-test for groups*

In one of the last sections, we compared the wages of college graduates with those of other workers, and noticed that graduates earned more money on average. Now there are two possibilities: either this difference is completely random and due to our (bad?) sample, or this difference is "real" and we would get the same result if we interviewed the entire population of women in the USA, instead of just our sample of about 2,200 people. To test this statistically, we can use a t-test for mean comparison by groups. The null hypothesis of the test is that both groups have the same mean values, while the alternative hypothesis is that the mean values actually differ (when you do not understand this jargon, please refer to your statistics textbook[10]).

---

10 There you will also learn that this test needs certain assumptions fulfilled to yield valid results. We just assume that this is the case here. In a research paper you should make sure that these assumptions are actually true (Acock, 2014: 164–168).

We can run the t-test by typing

```
ttest wage, by(collgrad)
```

Two-sample t test with equal variances

Group	Obs	Mean	Std. Err.	Std. Dev.	[95% Conf. Interval]	
not coll	1,714	6.910561	.1276104	5.283132	6.660273	7.16085
college	532	10.52606	.2742596	6.325833	9.987296	11.06483
combined	2,246	7.766949	.1214451	5.755523	7.528793	8.005105
diff		-3.615502	.2753268		-4.155424	-3.07558

```
    diff = mean(not coll) - mean(college)                      t = -13.1317
Ho: diff = 0                                  degrees of freedom =     2244

    Ha: diff < 0                 Ha: diff != 0                  Ha: diff > 0
 Pr(T < t) = 0.0000       Pr(|T| > |t|) = 0.0000            Pr(T > t) = 1.0000
```

or click **Statistics → Summaries, tables, and tests → Classical tests of hypotheses → t test (mean-comparison test)** and choose **Two-sample using groups**.

You will receive a large table that summarizes what we have already seen from our own tables, plus some additional information. You can locate our alternative hypothesis (*Ha: diff != 0*, read: "The difference is not equal to zero". Note that this hypothesis does not specify a direction and is therefore a two-tailed hypothesis). Below, you can read *Pr(|T| > |t|) = 0.0000*. This tells us that the calculated p-value is equal to 0.0000, which is very low and indicates that your result is statistically significant.[11] Therefore, we conclude that the mean wages of the two groups do actually differ and there is a "real" effect that cannot be explained by chance. Note that this does not tell us why there is a difference or what causes it. It would be incorrect to state that wages differ across groups *due to* college education, as this correlation might be spurious. Just suppose that the real factor behind the difference is intelligence because intelligent people work smarter. Furthermore, only intelligent people are admitted to college. Even if the causal effect of college-education was zero, we would still find this difference in wages.

When you have more than two groups you cannot use the t-test introduced here to test for group differences but you can use regression models to do so (also have a look at page 89).

---

11 In statistics it is common to refer to p-values below 0.05 as "significant" and to any values below 0.01 as "highly significant".

4.13 Weighting*

Until now we have assumed that our data is from a simple random sample, that means every unit of the population has the same probability of getting into the sample. In our case, that implies every working woman in the USA in 1988 had the same chance of being interviewed. Sometimes samples are way more complex, and we want want to introduce a slightly more sophisticated yet common example.

Suppose that you interview people in a city and your focus is research on migration. You want to survey the city as a whole, but also get a lot of information about the migrants living there. From the official census data you know that 5% of all inhabitants are migrants. As you plan to interview 1000 people you would normally interview 50 migrants, but you want to have more information about migrants, so you plan to oversample this group by interviewing 100 migrants. That means you only get to interview 900 non-migrants to keep the interviewing costs the same. When you calculate averages for the entire city you introduce a bias, due to oversampling (for example, when migrants are younger on average than non-migrants).

To account for this, you weight your cases. Migrants receive a weight that makes each case "less important", all other cases will be counted as "more important". You can calculate weights by dividing the probability of being in the sample when using a random design, by the actual probability, that is in our case (the following code is a made up example and won't work with the NLSW88 dataset):

$$W_{migrant} = \frac{0.05}{0.10} = 0.5 \quad \text{and} \quad W_{non\text{-}migrant} = \frac{0.95}{0.90} = 1.056$$

Notice that the weight for migrants is below 1 while it is greater than 1 for non-migrants. You create a variable (*pw1*) which has the numerical value of 0.5 if a respondent is migrant, and 1.056 if a respondent is non-migrant. We can use this variable in combination with other commands, for example

```
generate pw1 = 0.5 if migrant == 1
replace pw1 = 1.056 if migrant == 0
summarize age [weight=pw1], detail
```
[12]

The weight is called a design weight as it was created in relation to the design of our sampling process. Refer to help files to check which commands can be used in combination with weighting. Refer to the Stata manual to learn about the svy-commands that were introduced to make weighting for highly complex or clustered samples possible (Hamilton, 2013: 107–122). For a practical guide see Groves et al. (2004): 321–328.

---

12 Some other commands (like *tabulate*) require you to use integer-weights. To achieve this we multiply each value by 100 to account for all decimal places of the non-migrant weight (*replace pw1 = pw1*100*).

Statistical significance

Researchers are usually quite happy when they find a "significant" result, but what does this mean?[13] This term has already popped up a few times and will become even more important in the following chapters. To understand it, one has to remind oneself that the data being used is in almost all cases a (random) sample from a much larger population. Whenever we find an effect in an analysis, so that a coefficient is different from zero, we have to ask: did we get this result because there is a *real* effect out there in the population, or just because we were lucky and our sample is somewhat special? Stated differently: we have to take the sampling error into account.

As we can never test this rigorously (which would require repeating the analysis using the entire population instead of just the sample), statisticians have developed some tools that help us in deciding whether an effect is *real*. Remember, there is always a factor of uncertainty left, but a p-value, which indicates whether a result is significant, helps a lot. Usually, we refer to p-values below a value of 0.05 as significant, which is just a convention and not written in stone.

A common interpretation for a p-value, say 0.01, is: assuming that the effect is zero *in reality* (if you tested the entire population, not just a sample), you would find the test-results you received (or an even more extreme result) in 1% of all repetitions of your study, due to random sampling error. As this error-rate is quite low, most researchers would accept that your findings are real (but there is still a slight chance that you are just really unlucky with your sample, so be careful!).

---

[13] To be more concrete: they want to find that the coefficient of a variable of interest is statistically different from zero (in a regression model).

5 Introduction to causal analysis

By now, you will have mastered the basics of Stata. I would call this part descriptive statistics: methods that allow you to summarize your data, to get a general overview about means, standard deviations and distributions. These statistics should be the first part of every serious research as a good description is the foundation of any advanced analysis. The topics in the following chapters will introduce advanced methods that will enable you to test more interesting hypotheses, and make claims about causal relationships. Interestingly, many researchers, and especially those with a background in statistics, often avoid the word "causal" in their papers and rather use terms like "related" or "associated" to describe their findings. Though this is humble in general, as a perfect and thorough explanation of causality is a major challenge, it often does not help researchers and especially policy-makers, as they need advice for creating useful interventions to tackle real-world problems. Luckily you will soon notice that causal analysis is not defined by new or fancy methods that have just been invented , but is rather about thinking in a causal framework to create theories, test hypothesis and explicate results. Therefore, even advanced Stata users, who are new to causal analysis, will profit well from reading this section.

5.1 Correlation and causation

Nearly every student has heard this already: correlation does not imply causation. This is absolutely correct, as sometimes there are things that covary (appear together), and one thing does not cause the other. A very popular example is the correlation between the number of storks and fertility in women: the higher the number of storks in a certain region, the higher the fertility rate in that region (Matthews, 2000). We could draw this association as follows (Figure 5.1):

Storks $\longleftrightarrow$ Fertility

Figure 5.1: A correlation.

Using directed arrows on both ends should imply correlation and not a causal relationship. This association is symmetrical, meaning that when we know one thing we can predict the other. This brings us to another important aspect, namely the difference between prediction and causation. Sometimes it is good enough to predict certain outcomes, even when we are not interested in causality. For example, a demographer might be interested in predicting the number of births for a certain region. He might use variables that are causally linked to the birth rate, like the number of

https://doi.org/10.1515/9783110617160-005

women, average income, family structure and so on. But, he could also use other variables, like the number of storks in that region, even when he knows that there is no causal relationship between this variable and fertility. As long as this is a stable correlation it might be good enough to improve his forecast.

In science prediction is often not good enough when it comes to developing interventions to manipulate reality in our favor. Whenever we see a correlation and cannot make any interventions to influence the result (outcome), we know for sure that it cannot be a causal relation. For example, breeding storks and, therefore, increasing their population in a given region will probably not increase human fertility. Researchers are often interested in finding causal relations, so that policy-makers can use this knowledge to solve problems. Therefore, whenever we encounter a certain correlation, firstly, we have to check whether this relation is causal or not. One way to solve this problem is to think about factors that cause both phenomena at the same time, which would create the bias. This can be done by thinking theoretically and using previous research results and common sense. When we find such a common cause, we call it a confounder. One definition of confounder is: a variable that simultaneously affects two (or more) other variables. In our case the confounder would be the degree of urbanization, which both affects number of storks and fertility. In rural areas the number of storks is higher, due to larger number of natural habitats and food sources. Also, we expect higher fertility rates in rural areas, probably due to different social structures, tighter knit communities or different family values. We can depict this relation with the following illustration (Figure 5.2):

Storks $\longleftarrow$ Urbanization $\longrightarrow$ Fertility

Figure 5.2: Urbanization as a confounder.

Note that we have removed the connection between storks and fertility, as we no longer believe that there is any causal relation (the correlation is still there, yet usually not drawn in causal diagrams). We could use this graph as a working hypothesis: there is no relationship between the number of storks and fertility rates after taking the effect of urbanization into account, which is usually called "controlling". Stated differently: after controlling for urbanization, there is no effect of number of storks on fertility (or vice versa). We will come back to this aspect at the end of this chapter, as it is a little technical. In the next section we will proceed with something we have already started here: causal graphs.

5.2 Causal graphs

In my opinion, the largest appeal of modern causal analysis lies in its simplicity. The main tool for creating and solving causal questions are causal graphs, also called directed acyclic graphs (DAGs), which are so intuitive that even a ten year old child could grasp them. The procedure is as follows: focus on one relation of interest, like the effect of X on Y (for example the effect of the number of storks on fertility). Now add all other variables that might somehow be related to these two variables. Asterisks are added to variables that are unmeasured (unobserved), and, therefore, not available for direct analysis. Now draw arrows between the variables. Each arrow is only allowed to point in one direction (the D in DAG). Feedback loops are not allowed (acyclic). That means, an arrow cannot point to the variable it originated from (self causation) and when an arrow points from A to B there cannot be an arrow from B to A.[1] Every arrow implies a causal relationship between two variables, pointing from the cause to the effect. Conversely, when there is no arrow between two variables this means that these variables are not related causally. Therefore, drawing or omitting arrows imply strong assumptions that should be considered carefully. You should draw arrows based on common sense, theoretical considerations and previous research results. The arrows can also imply the tentative causal relationships, which you assume, but want to test explicitly.

The graph from the stork example (Figure 5.2) is such a DAG, yet very simple. In reality these can be larger, yet should not be overwhelmingly complex. If in doubt, it is better to deconstruct a research project into smaller analyses, than trying to analyze the entire framework in one big model. For a more detailed introduction to causal graphs, see the excellent paper by Elwert (2013).

DAGs have two major functions in modern causal analysis: Firstly they enable you to directly decide whether your research question can be answered causally. If it turns out that central variables are missing, it could be the case that no unbiased causal effect can be estimated from your current data (not even with the most fancy methods). This helps you avoiding futile work, so you can focus on changing your research or, even better, collect more data to fill your gaps. Secondly, when you come to the conclusion that you can answer your question with the data available, looking at the DAG will tell you which variables are important in your analysis, and which you can safely ignore. Let's leave the storks behind and take a more elaborate (generic) example with the following DAG:

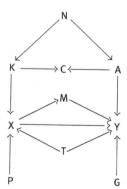

Figure 5.3: A more complex DAG.

---

1 This must also be the case on a more general level. Therefore the structure **A→B→C→A** is not allowed, as it is cyclic.

This one seems a little more complex than the example before, yet you will soon learn that there should be no problem dealing with it. Verify for yourself that this graph is acyclic, because there are no feedback loops and as long as you only follow the arrows in their direction you can never go back to the position you started from. Our goal is to estimate the causal effect of X on Y. Before we start talking about the general techniques to achieve this, I want to introduce certain constellations, that are famous in the literature, and will appear more often in real applications.

The confounder

We have talked about this constellation before, in Figure 5.2, as you will encounter it most often in applied research. Confounders, in the example above (Figure 5.3) are T, K, A or N , as all have multiple effects.[2] We will see that controlling for a confounder is often a good idea, to avoid bias, yet there are exceptions, so stay tuned.

The mechanism (mediator)

M is a mechanism in the example above (Figure 5.3), since the causal effect from X to Y is partially transmitted via this variable. Sometimes a mechanism can be the exclusive way for an effect transmission, meanwhile, as shown above, there are "leaking" ways around. A simple real-world example of a mechanism is a security alarm that goes off as soon as a window is broken. In this example, the causal diagram would look like this (Figure 5.4).

Intrusion ———⟶ Broken glass ———⟶ Alarm

Figure 5.4: Broken glass as a mediator.

The sensor that reacts when the glass is broken is the mediator, as it is the only way the alarm can be activated. If the burglar can pick the door and leaves the windows intact, the alarm will not go off. Mechanisms are often highly interesting phenomena when studied in detail. To stay with our example, when you finally find out that you had been burgled, but all the windows are intact, it is time to think about a better alarm system. Other examples of mechanisms are vitamin C, which mediates the effect of fruit intake on the outbreak of scurvy (epidemiology), and education, which mediates the effect of parental socioeconomic status on future income of children (sociology).

---

2 Technically, X is also a confounder in Figure 5.3, yet not labeled so, as it is part of the central cause-effect structure we are trying to analyze.

The collider

Probably the most non-intuitive constellation that has caused statisticians serious headaches for a long time is the collider, which is depicted by C in Figure 5.3 **(K→C←A)**. A collider is a variable that is caused by several other variables and is better left alone. What this means is that a collider usually does not bias your results, with the only exception that you control for it. Why is that the case? A simple real-world example: you visit a friend in a hospital that is specialized in heart and bone diseases. So there are only two possibilities for a patient: either his bones or his heart are not healthy (Figure 5.5).

Heart $\longrightarrow$ Admission $\longleftarrow$ Bone

Figure 5.5: Admission as a collider.

You cannot usually tell which sickness it is that leads to hospitalization. Now, you talk to a patient and she tells you that her heart is totally healthy. So you may conclude that she must have a disease of the bones, even when the two types of diseases are uncorrelated in the general population. Therefore, whenever you have a collider with the structure **(K→C←A)** and you control for C (for example by using C as a predictor variable in your regression model) variables K and A will no longer be independent of each other, which can introduce bias. For a more thorough introduction to colliders, see Elwert and Winship (2014).

After talking about these general structures it is time to come to the most interesting part, that is, using DAGs to estimate causal effects.

5.3 Estimating causal effects

You usually want to estimate the effect of variable X (cause, treatment, exposure) on Y (effect, outcome, result), for which you have drawn a causal graph as explained above. Now, it is time to see how this model guides you through the process of estimating the effect. First of all we address all causal pathways. A causal pathway is a path starting with an arrow pointing from the cause (X) to the outcome (Y), either directly **(X→Y)**, or with one or more mediating variables in-between **(X→M→Y)**. These are also called front-door paths. All other pathways are non-causal paths (causal and non-causal paths are defined relative to a specific cause and effect).

That brings us to non-causal pathways or back-door paths. A back-door path is a sequence of arrows, from cause to outcome, that starts with an arrowhead *towards* the cause (X) and finally ends at the outcome. For example, in Figure 5.3, **X←T→Y** is a back-door path. The arrow from T to X points towards X and, therefore, is a potential starting point for a back-door path. When you look along this line, you will reach T and from there you can reach Y. Another example of a back-door path is **X←K→C←A→Y**.

To estimate the unbiased causal effect of X on Y it is vital to close (block) all back-door paths between X and Y. How this can be done depends on the type of back-door. For example, the path **X←K→C←A→Y** is already blocked automatically , as any colliders on the path block the flow of information (as long as you do not control for them!). If there are confounders on the path, they will be blocked when you control for them. As long as we control for T, the back-door path **X←T→Y** will be blocked. The third and only remaining back-door path in the example is **X←K←N→A→Y**. This path does not contain a collider, therefore, it is unblocked. Luckily, you now have free choice: controlling for any variable of the path will block it. So you can control either for K, N or A. Note that the blocking should always be minimal, which means that you should only control for the lowest amount of variables necessary. When a path is already blocked controlling for more variables than actually needed might be harmful.

Let's take another generic example. Consider the causal graph depicted below (Figure 5.6). Again, you want to estimate the causal effect of X on Y. Identify all back-door paths and decide which variables you have to control to get an unbiased result.

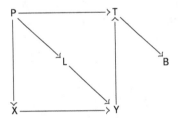

Figure 5.6: DAG Example 1.

Apparently there are two back-door paths: **X←P→L→Y** and **X←P→T←Y**. You will have noticed that T in the second path is a collider, so this path is blocked right from the start. Also note that B is a descendant of the collider T, therefore, controlling for B would be as harmful as controlling for T directly! The first path is open at the beginning, yet you have two options. You can either control for P or L, to block this path completely. This example also highlights that there can be back-door paths that have an arrow pointing away from the outcome (Y).

One last example. Consider the DAG below (Figure 5.7). Can you find a way of estimating the unbiased effect of X on Y? Consider that S* and H* are not measured, therefore, you cannot control for them.

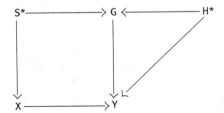

Figure 5.7: DAG Example 2.

When you scratch your head now, you might be right, as there is no way to estimate an unbiased effect with the data available. One back-door path goes from $X{\leftarrow}S^*{\rightarrow}G{\rightarrow}Y$, which can be blocked by controlling for G. But this is a problem, as controlling for G opens up another back-door path, namely $X{\leftarrow}S^*{\rightarrow}G{\leftarrow}H^*{\rightarrow}Y$.[3] Therefore it is impossible to estimate an unbiased effect, even with a million observations! The only way to solve this problem is to get back to the field and somehow measure either S or H. This should teach you two things: first, even with "Big data" it might be impossible to estimate causal effects when relevant variables are not measured. Second, drawing causal graphs can spare you a lot of futile work, because you can stop immediately when you encounter such a constellation in the conceptual phase. There is no need to waste any more resources on this task as you cannot estimate the unbiased causal effect (as was proven mathematically by Pearl (2009)). When you find my examples quite difficult, or have a more complex system of variables, you can also use free software that finds all back-door paths for you, and tells you which variables you have to control for (www.dagitty.net).

This concludes the introduction to causal graphs. Hopefully, you now have a feeling for how you can assess real life challenges, and start doing modern causal analysis. For further information on the topic, I refer you to the book of Pearl and Mackenzie (2018), which is suitable, even for the layperson. This was a very short primer, at least three other important techniques for estimating unbiased effects besides closing back-door paths were omitted, as these involve advanced knowledge. The front-door criterion and instrumental variables are introduced in a quite nontechnical fashion in the book of Morgan and Winship (2015). Do-calculus is presented and proven mathematically in Pearl (2009).

5.4 What does "controlling" actually mean?*

Statistical controlling, or just controlling, is one of the most central concepts in applied research. As we have learned above, not controlling for bias can easily distort our effects in various ways, which means that we might come to the wrong conclusions about how reality works. But what does controlling (also called conditioning or stratifying) mean in detail? I will explain this using a short example. Imagine we have data about a school (N=200) and some curious researcher notices a startling trend: weight and reading ability of children is related and heavier children tend to have higher scores on a reading test. Indeed, the statistical correlation is highly significant, therefore, we conclude that there is a "real" association. But what about

---

3 This example also shows that a variable can have different functions with respect to the pathway regarded. In the path $X{\leftarrow}S^*{\rightarrow}G{\rightarrow}Y$, G is a mediator, while it is a collider in the path $X{\leftarrow}S^*{\rightarrow}G{\leftarrow}H^*{\rightarrow}Y$.

causality? Is it possible that well fed children have more calories that can be used to power the brain, therefore, increasing the scores?[4] Actually, this correlation is spurious, as both factors are caused by the same aspect: the age of the child. Older children have better scores, as they have more reading experience and older children also have a higher weight, on average, as children still grow and become larger and heavier. Therefore, we have to include the confounder "age" in our model. We measure this by controlling for the class that the child is in (in this case, as age might not be available in the data, we say that the class a child is in is a good proxy for age, as pupils in elementary school are usually quite homogeneous within a class, with respect to age). To see how this works in detail we start with a scatterplot that visualizes the relation between reading scores and weight for all children in school.

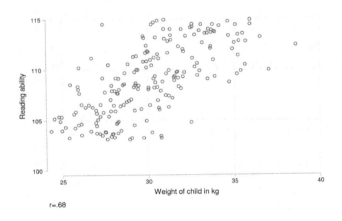

r=.68

We can clearly see that weight and reading are correlated and heavier children have better scores. What we do now is a perfect stratification on the variable of interest (class). Each stratum is defined by a class and we create new scatterplots, one for each class. By doing so we can see whether the general relation still holds.

Interestingly, the pattern vanished. When we look at children separated by class the association disappears and weight and reading ability are no longer related. Therefore, we can conclude that the correlation was spurious and age was the confounder. We could also calculate this numerically: first we calculate Pearson's R separately for each class, then we generate the weighted average (each class has 50 children in the example, therefore, we can just use the arithmetic mean without weighting). The result tells us that the correlation, after controlling for class (also called the partial correlation), is very low and not statistically significant.

---

4 We quietly ignore the possibility that children reading many hours every day tend to sit at their desks, which decreases energy consumption and, therefore, causes weight gain.

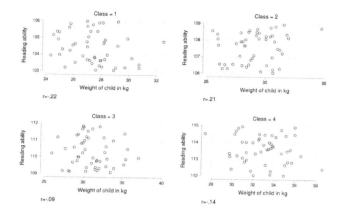

In the first example, age was operationalized, using the class a child was in, which allowed us to have a perfect stratification with four categories. But how does this work when the variable we want to control for is metric (continuous), for example, when age is measured as day since birth? We can assume that there are many "categories" and some of them might be empty (for example when no child has an age of exactly 3019 days). There are many ways to solve this problem. One quite simple option, which is used in linear regressions, is to use a linear approximation; therefore, it does not matter whether some categories are empty or sparsely populated, as long as enough data is available to estimate a linear function for reading ability and age.

You can see this as follows: start with the bivariate (2D) scatterplot which is depicted below. Suppose we draw a straight line through all the data points to estimate the linear function of the bivariate association. Now we include the control variable, and plot all three variables together. Each value (read, weight and age) describes one point in three-dimensional space. As we are now in 3D, we no longer fit a straight line, but a plane through the data (think of a sheet of paper that can be rotated and tilted, but not bent, until the optimal fit is reached). By doing this, it turns out that the first dimension (weight), is no longer relevant and the second (age) is much more important in devising the optimal fit (also see Pearl and Mackenzie (2018): 220–224).

One possibility to visualize this on printed paper is by using added-variable-plots. Again, we start with only two variables and use weight to predict reading ability (note that the variables were rescaled which explains the negative values) (Figure on the next page).

We see that there is a strong correlation between reading ability and weight, and Stata fitted the regression line for us. The slope is clearly positive (1.43). Does this relationship change when we include age (measured in days) as a control variable?

Absolutely. The fitted line is now almost horizontal, meaning that there is no slope, which is statistically different from zero, when age is included as a control variable. Our conclusion is that weight does not predict reading ability when the age of a child is also taken into account.

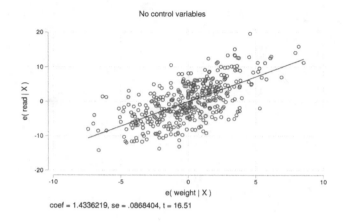

coef = 1.4336219, se = .0868404, t = 16.51

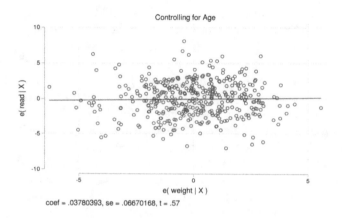

coef = .03780393, se = .06670168, t = .57

Hopefully this section helped you in understanding the basics of control variables. The specific techniques and formulas applied depend on the method used, and perfect stratification or linear approximations are only two of many possibilities, yet the general idea is often the same. Sometimes it does not even involve statistical methods at all, for example when controlling happens on the level of research design: when you plan to interview only a very specific subgroup of the population, this also implies controlling. Furthermore, this section should also underline the limits of controlling: when only very few cases have information on the control variable it might be challenging to fit a good approximation to a linear function. In other cases, the relationship between the outcome and the control is not linear, which poses great problems, as you will receive biased results if this is the case. The next chapters will tell you how you can deal with these problems, if they should arise in your own applications, and how to solve them.

6 Regression analysis

As we know how to manage and describe data we can go to the fun part and analyze data for our research. As this is an introduction to Stata, we will start with a method that is very popular and also a great foundation for the large family of regression-based applications. In this chapter we will learn how to run and interpret a multiple regression. In the next chapter we will furthermore check the most important assumptions that must hold, so our analyses will yield valid results.

6.1 Research question

Any good scientific research must start with a theoretically justified research question which has a relevance for the public. Finding a good research question, that is adequate for the scope of a term paper (15 pages or 8,000 words can be really short!), is a challenge, yet it is worth spending some time on this task, as your project (and grade) will really benefit from a well-formulated and manageable research question. Usually you start with a certain motivation in mind, and proceed with a literature review to check which questions are still open and find out where the interesting research gaps lie. You will then develop a theoretical framework, based on the previous literature and the general theoretical foundations of your field.

When this is done, you should formulate testable hypotheses that can be answered with the dataset you can access. This is the second crucial step, as it is easy to lose the focus and end up with hypotheses that are somewhat related to the research question, but vague and unclear. You really want to pinpoint a hypothesis, as your project will benefit by a clear and precise formulation. For a general overview of this process, refer to King et al. (1995): 3–28. Also try to formulate your research questions and hypotheses in a causal fashion, even when only observational data is available for analysis. As pointed out recently, almost all research is finally interested in causality and therefore, it is a good idea to spell this out explicitly (Hernán, 2018).

We imagine all this is done, so we can start with the analyses. Of course, as this book is short, we will deal with ad-hoc hypotheses to practice the methods. It should be clear that for any real seminar paper you should invest much more time in the mentioned aspects.

As we want to continue using our dataset of working women we will test the effects of certain variables on wage. We start by formulating testable hypotheses:
1. Union members will earn more than non-union members (H1).
2. People with more education will earn more than people with less education (H2).
3. The higher the total work experience, the higher the wage (H3).

https://doi.org/10.1515/9783110617160-006

As you might have noticed, our hypotheses use three different kinds of variable scalings: binary (H1), ordinal (H2) and metric (H3). Our dependent variable, that is the variable we want to explain, is metric (wage). When you want to use a linear (multiple) regression analysis, this must always be the case.[1]

6.2 What is a regression?

Linear regression[2] is a widely used statistical method to model the relationship between precisely one dependent variable (DV; the variable you want to explain or predict) and one or more independent (explaining) variables (IV). By including relevant control variables, researchers hope to furthermore *explain* the causal relationship between variables (as outlined in chapter five).

A regression produces an equation to describe the relationship between the variables in the model mathematically. Assuming we only have one IV, this would look something like

$$DV = \beta_0 + \beta_1 \cdot IV + \epsilon$$

where β_0 is the constant (also called intercept), β_1 the regression coefficient of the IV and ϵ is the error term. The error term "collects" the effect of all omitted variables that have an independent influence on your dependent variable, but are, as the term omitted describes, not captured in your model. Let's take an example. We want to regress income on motivation to see whether income can be explained by motivation. Our equation would look like this (with made up numbers):

$$Income = 400 + 20 \cdot motivation$$

This would mean that a person with a motivation of zero (whatever this means depends on your coding system) would earn 400, and every point more on the motivation scale would increase the income by 20. When your motivation is 10 you would receive an income of $400 + 20 \cdot 10 = 600$

Normally you would also include the error term in the equation, which is all the influence that cannot be explained by the model. For example, we assume that

---

1 If your dependent variable is binary, ordinal or nominal, you can use logistic or multinomial regressions instead.
2 This chapter introduces linear OLS regressions. For a more detailed introduction refer to Best and Wolf (2015). Exercises that might be interesting for you after you read this chapter can be found in Rabe-Hesketh and Skrondal (2012): 60–69.

income cannot be explained using just motivation, as skill or intelligence seem further important factors that are not considered. Thus our prediction will have a certain error. Remember that in a real-world setting every model will have (hopefully only) a minor error, as all factors can never be totally accounted for.

6.3 Binary independent variable

In our first model we want to inspect the relationship between wage and being a union member. Remember that our independent variable is coded binary, where the numerical value 1 is given to people who are members. If not already open, load the data and run the regression:

```
sysuse nlsw88, clear          //Open dataset
regress wage i.union          //Run regression
```

Source	SS	df	MS			
Model	751.256803	1	751.256803			
Residual	31862.1856	1,876	16.9841074			
Total	32613.4424	1,877	17.3753023			

Number of obs	=	1,878
$F(1, 1876)$	=	44.23
Prob > F	=	0.0000
R-squared	=	0.0230
Adj R-squared	=	0.0225
Root MSE	=	4.1212

wage	Coef.	Std. Err.	t	P>|t|	[95% Conf. Interval]	
union						
union	1.469625	.2209702	6.65	0.000	1.036252	1.902999
_cons	7.204669	.1094804	65.81	0.000	6.989953	7.419385

or click **Statistics → Linear models and related → Linear regression**. Let's take a look at the command first. *Regress* is the regression command in Stata, followed by the dependent variable (the one we want to explain). Note that a regression can only have one dependent variable, but one or more independent variables. These follow directly after. We use factor variable notation to tell Stata how to deal with a binary variable. Binary, nominal or ordinal variables receive the prefix i. (optional for binary variables), which helps Stata to run the correct model. Continuous or metric variables receive the prefix c. (which is optional, but often helpful for getting a quick overview of the model).

Let's take a look at the output.

The upper left corner of the table shows the decomposition of explained variance. These numbers are used to calculate some other statistics, like R-squared, which is depicted on the right hand side. Usually you do not have to care about this part of the table, as one uses better indicators to assess the model. The more interesting statistics are found on the right hand side.

Number of obs is the number of cases used in your model. As listwise deletion is the standard, only cases will be used which have complete information on every variable in the model. For example, if you use ten IVs in your model and one person only has information about nine of these (and the last one has a missing value), then this person is not used in calculating the model.

F(1, 1876) is used to calculate the **Prob > F** value. This is an omnibus-test which checks whether your model, in general, explains the variance of the dependent variable. If this value is not significant (larger than 0.05), your independent variable(s) might not be related to your dependent variable at all, and you should probably refine your model. As long as this number is low your model seems fine (as in our case here).

R-squared is the percentage of the overall variance that is explained by your model. This value is quite low and tells us that when we want to predict wages, the variable union alone is not sufficient to reach satisfying results. Usually it is not a good idea to assess the quality of a model using only the explained variance, yet it gives you a rough impression of the model fit. Keep in mind that you can still test causal mechanisms, even if R-squared is quite low. You can calculate this statistic by hand using the information on the left ($751/32,613 = 0.023$).

Adj R-squared is the adjusted R-squared, which is corrected to account for some problems that R-squared introduces. R-squared will always become larger the more controls you include, even if you introduce "nonsensical" independent variables to the model. To "punish" this, adjusted R-squared corrects for the number of explaining variables used.

Root MSE is the square root of the Mean Square Error. This value can be interpreted as follows: if you were to predict the wage of a person, using only the information in the model (that is information about the union status), you would, on average, make an error of about 4.12 $. But keep in mind that this number depends on your model and should not be compared across different models.

The more interesting numbers are in the lower part, where the coefficients and significance levels are shown. We can formulate our regression equation, which would be

$$Wage = 7.2 + 1.47 \cdot Union$$

7.2 is the constant (or intercept), while 1.47 is the coefficient of our independent variable. As union can only take two values (0 and 1), there are only two possible results. Non-union members will have an average wage of 7.2 while union-members will have an average value of $7.2 + 1.47 = 8.67$. The p-value (P>|t|) of this coefficient is below 0.05, so we know the result is significant. Thus we conclude that there is a real effect of union membership on wages, and the result is positive. Please note that this result might be spurious, as there are no control variables in the model. Formulated differently, the effect may disappear when we introduce more explanatory variables to the model. We will deal with this in model 3.

6.4 Ordinal independent variable

After discussing the most simple case, we move on to a model with an ordinal independent variable. As there is no real ordinal variable in the dataset that could be used directly, we have to create one.[3] We will use the metric variable, years of schooling (grade), and transform it (low education, medium education, high education). After this is done, we use a crosstab to inspect if we made any mistakes.

```
recode grade (0/10 = 1 "low education") ///
    (11/13 = 2 "medium education") ///
    (14/18 = 3 "high education"), generate(education)⁴
```

tabulate grade education   //Check results

current grade completed	RECODE of grade (current grade completed)			Total
	low educa	medium ed	high educ	
0	2	0	0	2
4	3	0	0	3
5	1	0	0	1
6	14	0	0	14
7	19	0	0	19
8	33	0	0	33
9	55	0	0	55
10	84	0	0	84
11	0	123	0	123
12	0	943	0	943
13	0	176	0	176
14	0	0	187	187
15	0	0	92	92
16	0	0	252	252
17	0	0	106	106
18	0	0	154	154
Total	211	1,242	791	2,244

Lowering the metric of a scale should always be justified on a theoretical base, as information is lost in the process, yet it can be a valuable technique to adapt available variables to theoretical concepts. After this is done, we run our model using the created variable.

---

3 Note that we create an ordinal variable for the sake of demonstration for this example but we will use the metric version for the rest of chapter six and seven, so working through the book is more convenient.

4 Note that this categorization is data driven to assure that all groups end up with a sufficient number of cases. In real research, creating categories should probably be justified on a theoretical basis.

```
regress wage i.education
```

Source	SS	df	MS		Number of obs	=	2,244
					F(2, 2241)	=	120.80
Model	7236.00472	2	3618.00236		Prob > F	=	0.0000
Residual	67118.3258	2,241	29.9501677		R-squared	=	0.0973
					Adj R-squared	=	0.0965
Total	74354.3305	2,243	33.1495009		Root MSE	=	5.4727

wage	Coef.	Std. Err.	t	P>|t|	[95% Conf. Interval]	
education						
medium education	1.903661	.4075026	4.67	0.000	1.104539	2.702783
high education	5.212161	.4240373	12.29	0.000	4.380614	6.043708
_cons	4.87799	.3767545	12.95	0.000	4.139166	5.616814

Stata's factor variable notation makes our life much easier. Usually any ordinal or nominal variable has be to be recoded into dummy variables to be used in regressions. For example, we would have to recode our variable education into two binary variables, "medium_education" and "high_education". One category (in this case, "low_education") would be our reference-category. Luckily we can skip this step by using a Stata shortcut.

As the category low education is our reference, we find this effect in the constant. A person with low education will earn 4.88 on average. A person with medium education will make 1.90 more than that (4.88 + 1.90), a person with high education 5.21 more (4.88 + 5.21). All variables are highly significant, telling us that in comparison to low education, the two other groups make a significant difference. We would thus conclude that education has a positive effect on wage, and education pays off financially. Also note that our R-squared is higher than in the first model, telling us that education can explain more variation of wage than the membership in a union.

Stata will always use the category within a variable with the lowest numerical value as a reference category. You can show the category of reference explicitly by typing

```
set showbaselevels on, perm⁵
```

before running your regression command.

When you want to change your category of reference, recode the independent variable or use an option for the factor variable notation.

---

5 The option *perm* makes this configuration permanent, so you do not have to enter this command every time you start Stata.

```
regress wage ib3.education
```

Source	SS	df	MS		
Model	7236.00472	2	3618.00236		
Residual	67118.3258	2,241	29.9501677		
Total	74354.3305	2,243	33.1495009		

Number of obs	=	2,244
F(2, 2241)	=	120.80
Prob > F	=	0.0000
R-squared	=	0.0973
Adj R-squared	=	0.0965
Root MSE	=	5.4727

wage	Coef.	Std. Err.	t	P>|t|	[95% Conf. Interval]	
education						
low education	-5.212161	.4240373	-12.29	0.000	-6.043708	-4.380614
medium education	-3.308501	.2489541	-13.29	0.000	-3.796705	-2.820296
high education	0	(base)				
_cons	10.09015	.1945859	51.85	0.000	9.708564	10.47174

Here category three (high education) would be the reference. You will notice that all coefficients will change. This must happen since all your relative comparisons will change as well. Someone with low education will have a wage of 10.09 − 5.21 = 4.88, which is exactly the same value, as calculated above. You see that changing the reference categories of independent variables does not change results. You should choose them in a fashion that helps you understand the results.

What about ANOVAs?

Analysis of variance (ANOVA) is a quite popular method in psychology, and some readers might wonder why it is not included in the book. The answer is that ANOVAs are very similar to OLS regressions and internally Stata uses regression algorithms when calculating ANOVAs. Furthermore, you can always "simulate" an ANOVA with a regression model, while this is not possible the other way round. My personal advice is that, although many courses start with ANOVAs, you can directly use regression models and get the same results while keeping all your options open when it comes to advanced analyses, which can be built on your initial model.

But let's start simply. Usually an ANOVA is used to determine whether there are any differences in a metric variable, between three or more groups. In our example, we test whether blood pressure is different for three groups which are defined by the age of participants. You can think of an ANOVA as a more general version of a t-test (see page 69) which tells you whether there are any differences in the mean outcome for an arbitrary number of groups. When the result is significant you know that at least two groups show a statistically significant difference in the means. We can run an example by using another dataset (so make sure to save your current results before typing the next commands!):

```
sysuse bpwide, clear          //Open new example dataset
oneway bp_before agegrp, tabulate    //Run ANOVA
```

Age Group	Summary of Before Mean	Std. Dev.	Freq.
30-45	151.675	9.2580872	40
46-59	155.1	11.459628	40
60+	162.575	10.727122	40
Total	156.45	11.389845	120

Source	Analysis of Variance SS	df	MS	F	Prob > F
Between groups	2485.55	2	1242.775	11.23	0.0000
Within groups	12952.15	117	110.702137		
Total	15437.7	119	129.728571		

Bartlett's test for equal variances: chi2(2) =   1.7863 Prob>chi2 = 0.409

or click **Statistics → Linear models and related → ANOVA/MANOVA → One-way ANOVA.**

The command runs the ANOVA, where your dependent variable (which has to be continuous) is blood pressure and the groups are defined by the second variable, agegrp. The option *tabulate* displays the means and standard deviations for each group. You can also obtain all pairwise contrasts when you include the option *bonferroni*.

In the upper part of the table you see the means for each group, which already tell us that at least one difference seems quite large (151.7 VS 162.6). The interesting part, in the next section of the output, is the result under **Prob > F**, which is smaller than 0.05 and therefore, indicates that the result is significant. We conclude that at least two groups show a statistically significant difference in the means. Bartlett's test indicates a non significant result (Prob>chi2 = 0.409), which is good, otherwise we would have to conclude that variances between the groups were unequal. This would violate the assumptions of the ANOVA.

You can easily come to the same conclusions using a regression model. Just type:

```
regress bp_before i.agegrp
```

Source	SS	df	MS		Number of obs	=	120
					F(2, 117)	=	11.23
Model	2485.55	2	1242.775		Prob > F	=	0.0000
Residual	12952.15	117	110.702137		R-squared	=	0.1610
					Adj R-squared	=	0.1467
Total	15437.7	119	129.728571		Root MSE	=	10.522

bp_before	Coef.	Std. Err.	t	P>|t|	[95% Conf. Interval]	
agegrp						
46-59	3.425	2.352681	1.46	0.148	-1.234361	8.084361
60+	10.9	2.352681	4.63	0.000	6.240639	15.55936
_cons	151.675	1.663597	91.17	0.000	148.3803	154.9697

Using the i. prefix tells Stata to treat agegrp as a categorical variable. At the top of the output you see the F-statistic and Prob > F, which are identical to the ones displayed by the ANOVA (11.23 and 0.0000). You can also see more detailed results when you check the lower parts of the output. The first category

(30–45) is used as a reference and therefore, not shown in the table. We learn that the third group (60+) displays a highly significant result (P>|t| is smaller than 0.05 here), therefore, we conclude that there is a difference from the reference-group.

What if you want to test if age-group 2 (46–59) is statistically different from age-group 3 (60+)? You have several possibilities: firstly you could change the category of reference in the regression model (see page 89). Secondly, you can use the *test* command to test this numerically:

```
test 2.agegrp = 3.agegrp          //Output omitted
```

You can find this test under **Statistics → Postestimation → Test, contrasts, and comparisons of parameter estimates** and click **Create**. As the result (0.0019) is significant (Prob > F is smaller than 0.05) you know that the two group means are different from each other.

In summary, you should keep in mind that ANOVAs and linear regressions are very similar from a technical point of view, while regressions are more versatile and powerful for advanced analyses, hence, the emphasis on these models in the rest of the book.

6.5 Metric independent variable

Lastly, we want to use a metric (continuous) explanatory variable. We type

```
regress wage c.ttl_exp
```

Source	SS	df	MS		Number of obs	=	2,246
					F(1, 2244)	=	170.14
Model	5241.29609	1	5241.29609		Prob > F	=	0.0000
Residual	69126.6713	2,244	30.805112		R-squared	=	0.0705
					Adj R-squared	=	0.0701
Total	74367.9674	2,245	33.1260434		Root MSE	=	5.5502

wage	Coef.	Std. Err.	t	P>|t|	[95% Conf.	Interval]
ttl_exp	.3314291	.0254087	13.04	0.000	.2816021	.3812562
_cons	3.612492	.3393469	10.65	0.000	2.947026	4.277959

The table shows a highly significant effect, with a numerical value of 0.33, and 3.61 for the constant. Thus a person with zero years total work experience would earn 3.61\$ on average, and with each year more she would receive 0.33\$ more. Therefore, a person with five years of education would earn $3.61 + 5 \cdot 0.33 = 5.26$ Note this is the case, as work experience is coded in years. If we used months instead, all the numbers would be different, but the actual effects would stay the same. We conclude that the effect of work experience on wage is positive, which makes sense intuitively, as experience should be beneficial for workers.

In chapter five we learned that controlling for the correct variables is essential when we want to recover causal effects. We will do this by including some more variables: union status, place of residence (south VS other) and years of education (as a metric variable). Therefore, our final (saturated) model is estimated with the following command[6]:

```
regress wage c.ttl_exp i.union i.south c.grade
```

Source	SS	df	MS			
				Number of obs	=	1,876
				F(4, 1871)	=	198.53
Model	9714.24396	4	2428.56099	Prob > F	=	0.0000
Residual	22887.2306	1,871	12.2326192	R-squared	=	0.2980
				Adj R-squared	=	0.2965
Total	32601.4745	1,875	17.3874531	Root MSE	=	3.4975

wage	Coef.	Std. Err.	t	P>|t|	[95% Conf. Interval]	
ttl_exp	.266036	.0178493	14.90	0.000	.2310294	.3010426
union						
union	.8229425	.1905739	4.32	0.000	.4491827	1.196702
1.south	-1.011447	.1658579	-6.10	0.000	-1.336733	-.686161
grade	.5909214	.03243	18.22	0.000	.5273186	.6545242
_cons	-3.392946	.463591	-7.32	0.000	-4.302156	-2.483737

Note that the coefficient of work experience became slightly smaller, yet is still highly significant. R-squared also increased drastically, as our model with four independent variables is able to explain much more variance in wages. One could interpret our results as follows: "the effect of work experience on wage is highly significant and each year more experience will result in a wage plus of 0.27$ on average , when controlling for union-membership, region and years of education". Usually it is not necessary to explain the effect of every single control variable, as you are interested in one special effect. Note that we call a model with more than one independent variable a multiple regression.

It is worth taking some time to understand the correct interpretation of the result. The positive effect of work experience is independent of all other variables in the model, which are: union status, region and education. Or to formulate it differently: every extra year of work experience increases the wage by 0.27$, when holding all other variables in the model constant (ceteris paribus interpretation). When you build your model using the framework of causal analysis, and have selected the correct variables to control for (closing all back-door paths), you could even state that work experience is a cause of income (which is probably wrong in our example, as we have not done all the important steps, and have created an ad-hoc model to give as a general example).

---

6 The order of the independent variables is without any meaning and does not influence the results.

In chapter ten we will continue to interpret and visualize effects that we have estimated using regressions so far. Finally, it is time to come back to our hypotheses and see whether our results do support or reject them.

H1 claims that union members will earn more than non-union members. As the coefficient of the variable union is positive, and the p-value highly significant (page 85), we can state: union members do, on average, earn more money than non-union members. We therefore, accept hypothesis one.[7]

H2 claims that more educated people will earn more money. We can state: people with a higher education do earn more money on average, as, in contrast to the lowest category of education, both other coefficients show a positive and highly significant result (page 88). We therefore, accept hypothesis two.

H3 claims that people with more work experience earn more money. We can state: as the coefficient for work experience is positive and highly significant, people with more work experience do earn more money on average after controlling for union membership, region and education (page 92). We therefore, accept hypothesis three.

Confidence intervals

Confidence intervals are a common type of interval estimation for expressing uncertainty in a statistic. In the regression commands so far you have seen that Stata also reports a confidence interval for each coefficient. The problem is that we (mostly) work with samples from a much greater population, that means all statistics we calculate are probably not identical to the result we would get if we could use all cases that exist. For example, our sample consists of working women between 34 and 46 years of age. We want to know the average work experience they have, which yields 12.53 years (*summarize ttl_exp*). Suppose we not only have a sample, but interview every single woman in the USA between 34 and 46. We would then probably get a different result and not 12.53. A confidence interval tries to give us a measurement, to see how much trust we can put in our statistic. To compute it, just type

ci means ttl_exp

Variable	Obs	Mean	Std. Err.	[95% Conf. Interval]	
ttl_exp	2,246	12.53498	.0972782	12.34421	12.72574

---

7 Keep in mind that you can never *verify* a hypothesis, as, strictly speaking, they can only be rejected. If we cannot reject an hypothesis, we *accept* it (for the time being, as new data or insights could change our views in the future). If you are interested in this topic, I refer you to the writings of Karl Popper.

or click **Statistics → Summaries, tables, and tests → Summary and descriptive statistics → Confidence intervals**. The standard is a 95% interval. The standard error of the mean is 0.097, the calculated confidence interval is [12.34; 12.73]. Be careful with the interpretation, as many people get it wrong and it is even printed incorrectly in journal articles (Hoekstra, Morey, Rouder, Wagenmakers, 2014)! A correct interpretation would be: "If we were to redraw the sample over and over, 95% of the time, the confidence intervals contain the *true* mean."[8] Of course, our sample must consist of a random sample of the population for this statement to be valid. When we know that our sample is biased, say we only interviewed people from New York, then the entire statistic is biased.

To understand the interpretation, remember that there must be a true value for our statistic, which we would know if we had interviewed not a sample, but every single person. Imagine we went out and collected a sample, not only once, but 100 times, independently. Then in 95 of these 100 samples the calculated confidence interval would contain the true value. In five of the samples it would not. Also, remember that a confidence interval gets *larger* when we increase the level. That is why a 99% confidence interval for work experience would be [12.28; 12.79] and thus broader than the one calculated before. To see why this is true, consider the extreme case, a 100% confidence interval. As this *must* include the true value it has to be from zero to infinity!

TL;DR[9]: Never use this interpretation: ~~"the probability, that the true value is contained in the interval, is 95%."~~

6.6 Interaction effects*

Until now we have assumed that all effects have the same strength for all persons. For example, the effect of work experience on wage is 0.27, no matter whether you are a union member or not, whether you are from the south, or not, or whatever your education is. We call this the average effect of experience and often this is good enough. But sometimes we think, based on our theoretical reasoning, that there are subgroups which are affected quite differently by some variables. For example, we could argue that there is an interaction effect between being union members and having college education, with respect to wages. Stated differently, we expect that the possession of a college degree moderates how union-membership affects income. In this example union-membership is the main effect, while college education is the interaction effect. Finally, it is recommended you to draw a causal graph of the model, which could look like this (Figure 6.1):

---

8 In fact, researchers discuss whether only this very strict interpretation is correct, especially as this is a question about how one views statistics (Frequentist VS Bayesian approach), see http://rynesherman. com/blog/misinterpreting-confidence-intervals/ (2018-01-26).
9 "Too long; didn't read"

College Education   **Figure 6.1:** An interaction effect

Interaction effects might sound complicated at first, but are very common in data analysis, and it is very useful to take some time and make sure that you really understand what this means. Due to factor variable notation it is very easy to calculate these effects in Stata. Generally, it is recommended you have a three stage procedure: Your first model only includes the main effect. The second model includes the main effect, all control variables and also the interaction variable, but without the interaction effect itself. Finally, the third model furthermore adds the interaction effect. As we want to keep it simple and only specify total work experience as a control variable, we would run these three models:

```
regress wage i.union                         //M1 (Output omitted)
regress wage i.union i.collgrad c.ttl_exp    //M2 (Output omitted)
regress wage i.union##i.collgrad c.ttl_exp   //M3
```

Source	SS	df	MS		Number of obs	=	1,878
					F(4, 1873)	=	160.31
Model	8317.90759	4	2079.4769		Prob > F	=	0.0000
Residual	24295.5348	1,873	12.9714548		R-squared	=	0.2550
					Adj R-squared	=	0.2535
Total	32613.4424	1,877	17.3753023		Root MSE	=	3.6016

wage	Coef.	Std. Err.	t	P>|t|	[95% Conf. Interval]	
union						
union	1.267032	.2309937	5.49	0.000	.8139994	1.720064
collgrad						
college grad	3.398876	.2308588	14.72	0.000	2.946109	3.851644
union#collgrad						
union#college grad	-.9363669	.4266358	-2.19	0.028	-1.773098	-.0996353
ttl_exp	.294504	.0181619	16.22	0.000	.2588843	.3301236
_cons	2.713367	.2501927	10.85	0.000	2.222682	3.204053

By typing two hash signs (##) between i.union and i.collgrad you tell Stata to calculate the main effects of union-membership, the main effect of college education and additionally the interaction effect between both. When you just type a single hash - sign, Stata will only calculate the interaction effect, which is usually not what we want. Again, the order of the independent variables is arbitrary. Also note that this notation is symmetric. Stata does not know which variable is the "main" and which is the interaction as, from a mathematical point of view, this cannot be distinguished. It is up to you to define and interpret the results in a way you desire, just like we did in Figure 6.1.

In the following I will show different options on how to interpret and visualize the results. Which option seems most comfortable is up to you.

6.6.1 The classic way

First, we will use the output of the model and interpret results directly, which can be slightly challenging. We see that the coefficient of union is positive and highly significant (1.27), telling us that union-members earn more on average than non-members. Exactly the same is true for college education (3.40). Finally, we see that the interaction effect (−0.936) is negative and also significant (p-value smaller than 0.05). We can now calculate the overall effect of union-membership for two groups, the people with college education and those without.

$$Effect \text{ (union}|non - college) = 1.27 + (-0.936) \cdot collegeeducation = 1.27 + 0 = 1.27^{10}$$
$$Effect \text{ (union}|college) = 1.27 + (-0.936) \cdot collegeeducation = 1.27 - 0.936 = 0.334$$

Here we calculate the effect of union-membership for both groups, using the classic way. Our conclusion is that the effect is much stronger for people without college, which means that people with less education profit more from union-memberships. You have noticed that this procedure requires you to calculate effects by hand, which becomes rapidly more complex as soon as more variables or other interactions are present. Therefore, we would kindly ask Stata to do this for us.

6.6.2 Marginal effects

Using *margins* we can calculate marginal effects of union-membership easily, which are the effects for the two groups (people with college education VS people without college education). Therefore, we run

---

10 Read: "The effect of union-membership given non-college education". In our example college education can only have two values, zero or one, therefore, only two equations are necessary. If you have an interaction with a variable with more categories, you have to calculate the effect for all values. If your interaction-variable has a metric scale (like age), it is often a good idea to summarize it into a few ordinal categories (for example young people, medium aged people and older people).

```
margins, dydx(union) at(collgrad=(0 1))
```

```
Average marginal effects                          Number of obs    =    1,878
Model VCE    : OLS

Expression     : Linear prediction, predict()
dy/dx w.r.t. : 1.union

1._at          : collgrad        =        0

2._at          : collgrad        =        1
```

	dy/dx	Delta-method Std. Err.	t	P>|t|	[95% Conf. Interval]	
0.union	(base outcome)					
1.union _at						
1	1.267032	.2309937	5.49	0.000	.8139994	1.720064
2	.3306647	.3587427	0.92	0.357	-.3729127	1.034242

Note: dy/dx for factor levels is the discrete change from the base level.

If you want to use point-and-click, go to **Statistics → Postestimation → Marginal analysis → Marginal means and marginal effects**.

This command tells Stata to calculate the marginal effect of union-membership (the dydx-option), separately for people with college education (collgrad = 1) and people without (collgrad = 0). Note that we run this command directly after the model and that we do not have to specify anything else, because Stata regards the factor-variable notation and includes the interaction. The results are what we calculated manually (differences are due to rounding). Therefore, we come to the same results, minus the trouble of calculating it ourselves. Also keep in mind that, strictly speaking, union-membership has only a significant effect for the people without college education, as this p-value is very low and below 0.05. The p-value for the other group is much higher (0.357), telling us that this coefficient is probably not statistically different from zero. Therefore, there is no real effect left for this group.

6.6.3 Predicted values

Another option I want to introduce here does not emphasize *effects* of certain variables, but rather uses all information in the model (therefore, also the data from the control variables) to predict the overall *outcomes* for certain groups (which implicitly also tells us something about effects or differences between groups). Again, we can use *margins* here:

```
margins, at(union = (0 1) collgrad=(0 1))
```

```
Predictive margins                              Number of obs    =     1,878
Model VCE    : OLS

Expression   : Linear prediction, predict()
1._at        : union            =            0
               collgrad         =            0
2._at        : union            =            0
               collgrad         =            1
3._at        : union            =            1
               collgrad         =            0
4._at        : union            =            1
               collgrad         =            1
```

	Margin	Delta-method Std. Err.	t	P>|t|	[95% Conf. Interval]	
_at						
1	6.488428	.1087936	59.64	0.000	6.275058	6.701797
2	9.887304	.2031015	48.68	0.000	9.488975	10.28563
3	7.755459	.2036173	38.09	0.000	7.356119	8.1548
4	10.21797	.2964678	34.47	0.000	9.636527	10.79941

Stata directly calculates expected wages and also regards the effect of work experience. For example, a person who is not in a union and, also holds no college degree, would earn 6.49$ on average. When you want to compare results between groups, make sure you get the correct comparisons. In this case, we would compare group 1 VS 3 (no college education) and group 2 VS 4 (college education) to assess the effect of union-membership on wages. You can also get a visual output by typing

```
marginsplot
```

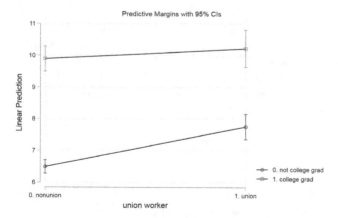

Again, we come to the conclusion that the effect of union-membership is moderated by degree of education. Union-membership has a quite strong effect for people without college education, but a much lower effect for highly educated people.

Margins is a very powerful command that we will use in chapter ten to visualize our results. When you still feel insecure about interactions, don't be discouraged, as *margins* makes it simple to get informative results, even when there are many interactions present in your model. If our model was slightly more complex, even experts would not calculate these effects by hand, but use the Stata internals to get nice graphics that can be interpreted visually.

6.6.4 Separate analyses by subgroups

A final technique for dealing with interactions is to run separate regressions for each subpopulation, which is defined by your interaction variable. In the example above, our interacting variable is college education, which means we have two groups: people who have college education and people without college education. We can remove the interacting variable from our regression model and instead run two models, the first for people with college education, the second for people without.

```
bysort collgrad: regress wage i.union c.ttl_exp
```

```
-> collgrad = not college grad
```

Source	SS	df	MS		Number of obs	=	1,414
					F(2, 1411)	=	161.25
Model	3254.28865	2	1627.14433		Prob > F	=	0.0000
Residual	14238.2776	1,411	10.0909126		R-squared	=	0.1860
					Adj R-squared	=	0.1849
Total	17492.5663	1,413	12.3797355		Root MSE	=	3.1766

wage	Coef.	Std. Err.	t	P>|t|	[95% Conf. Interval]	
union						
union	1.270282	.2037895	6.23	0.000	.870519	1.670045
ttl_exp	.2894086	.0175682	16.47	0.000	.254946	.3238712
_cons	2.77661	.2381435	11.66	0.000	2.309457	3.243763

```
-> collgrad = college grad
```

Source	SS	df	MS		Number of obs	=	464
					F(2, 461)	=	15.83
Model	690.147498	2	345.073749		Prob > F	=	0.0000
Residual	10052.2226	461	21.805255		R-squared	=	0.0642
					Adj R-squared	=	0.0602
Total	10742.3701	463	23.2016632		Root MSE	=	4.6696

wage	Coef.	Std. Err.	t	P>|t|	[95% Conf. Interval]	
union						
union	.3284987	.4651464	0.71	0.480	-.5855714	1.242569
ttl_exp	.3196297	.0573476	5.57	0.000	.2069347	.4323248
_cons	5.770544	.8229523	7.01	0.000	4.153341	7.387747

To understand what *bysort* does, see how we can get the exact same results with the if qualifier:

```
regress wage i.union c.ttl_exp if collgrad == 0
regress wage i.union c.ttl_exp if collgrad == 1
```

- output omitted -

By comparing the coefficients of union, you can check whether there is any interaction. When the coefficients are quite similar, we would conclude that there is no interaction at all. In our case the results underline that there are differences (1.27 for people without college, 0.33 for people with college). You will notice that these results are very close to what we have calculated above as "marginal effects". This split-technique is preferred when you have many variables in the model, and you expect many interaction effects. For example, when you expect interactions, not only between union and college, but also between total work experience and college, you would normally have to specify the second effect in another interaction-term. When you run separate regressions by groups, the model will implicitly account for any possible interactions between your grouping variable and any other explaining variable used in the model. Basically, this design can be helpful when you expect your groups to be highly different from each other in a large number of effects. If necessary, you could even specify explicit interactions, within this split-design, to account for higher orders of interaction (if there is any theoretical expectation of this). The main downside of this split approach is that your two groups are no longer in the same model, therefore you cannot compare coefficients easily. For example, it is no longer possible to tell if the coefficient of experience in model one (0.289) is statistically different from the same coefficient in model two (0.32).

To summarize this section, interaction effects are often highly interesting and central to many research questions. Possible examples are: that a drug has different effects on men and women, a training program affects young and old workers differently, or a newly introduced tax influences spending of large and small firms differently. Whenever you want to test interactions, you should have a clear theoretical framework in mind that predicts different outcomes. Thanks to Stata, actually calculating and interpreting interactions is as easy as can be.

6.7 Standardized regression coefficients*

Standardized regression coefficients, or beta coefficients, are quite popular in some disciplines. They basically have two applications: firstly, they make it possible to compare different studies which try to explain the same phenomena but use different units of measurement (for example, one study measures time in days, while the other in months). Secondly, they make it possible to compare effect-sizes for variables with different units within one study (for example, when you want to measure what affects life satisfaction more, the income or the number of close friends). The idea is as follows: you z-standardize (see the formula in the footnote on page 49) your dependent variable and all (metric) independent variables and use these modified variables in your regression. Stata makes this easy:

```
regress wage c.ttl_exp, beta
```

Source	SS	df	MS			
				Number of obs	=	2,246
				F(1, 2244)	=	170.14
Model	5241.29609	1	5241.29609	Prob > F	=	0.0000
Residual	69126.6713	2,244	30.805112	R-squared	=	0.0705
				Adj R-squared	=	0.0701
Total	74367.9674	2,245	33.1260434	Root MSE	=	5.5502

wage	Coef.	Std. Err.	t	P>|t|	Beta
ttl_exp	.3314291	.0254087	13.04	0.000	.2654767
_cons	3.612492	.3393469	10.65	0.000	.

The output shows the normal coefficient (0.331) and the standardized coefficient (0.265). The interpretation is as follows: when the work experience of a woman increases by one standard deviation, the wage increases by 0.265 standard deviations. The result is highly significant.

If you would like to see how this works in detail, you can reproduce the results on your own:

```
quietly sum wage
generate zwage = (wage-r(mean))/r(sd)
quietly sum ttl_exp
generate zttl_exp = (ttl_exp-r(mean))/r(sd)
regress zwage c.zttl_exp
```

You see that the results are identical. When you want to learn more about standardized coefficients in Stata, have a look at the paper by Doug Hemken.[11]

---

[11] https://www.ssc.wisc.edu/~hemken/Stataworkshops/stdBeta/Getting%20Standardized%20Coefficients%20Right.pdf (2018-05-11)

7 Regression diagnostics

There are some assumptions that must be fulfilled, so the regression will yield correct results (Wooldridge, 2016: 73–83; Meuleman, Loosveldt, Emonds, 2015). Therefore, it is strongly recommended to test these assumptions to see whether you can trust your conclusions. When you find out that there are great problems in the data, it might be a good idea to redo analyses, or find other data sources. The least you can do is report all the violations, so others can regard this when reading your paper.

If not otherwise stated, all diagnostics are applied to the following model we used in chapter six:

```
sysuse nlsw88, clear
regress wage c.ttl_exp i.union i.south c.grade
```

7.1 Exogeneity

The term exogeneity describes that the expected error, given all your independent variables, must be zero.[1] Stated differently, any knowledge about your independent variables does not give you any information about the error term. When we come back to our example from the last chapter, this means that a union member has the same intelligence, motivation, etc... as a non-union member, unless these variables are also used as controls in the model.

This is a very strict assumption that cannot be tested statistically. When you want to pinpoint causal effects with your analyses, you have to make sure that you account for all possible further explanations, which is a difficult task. Refer to introductions to causal analysis, to learn more about that (see chapter five in this book, Morgan and Winship (2015) and De Vaus (2001)). For the moment, you should keep in mind that when you think that several other factors could have a causal influence on your dependent variable (that are in any way connected to one of your explaining (IV) variables), you have to control for these factors.

To summarize, there is no statistical test that tells you whether your model is "correct" and will calculate the desired causal effect. Nevertheless, there is one test you can try, the Ramsey test, to see whether there are general problems with the model.

```
estat ovtest
```

```
Ramsey RESET test using powers of the fitted values of wage
      Ho:  model has no omitted variables
               F(3, 1868) =      11.82
                Prob > F =       0.0000
```

---

[1] Or as a formula: $E(\epsilon \mid IV_1, IV_2, ..., IV_k) = E(\epsilon) = 0$

https://doi.org/10.1515/9783110617160-007

or click **Statistics** → **Postestimation** → **Reports and statistics** and choose **Ramsey regression specification-error test**.

If the p-value (**Prob > F**) is smaller than 0.05, then there are either important missing variables, or useless ones included in your model. As you see in the example, this is actually the case for our model (which is no big surprise, as this is an ad hoc demonstration which lacks any deeper theoretical justification). When you get such results, try to find other important variables that might help to explain your causal effects, and rethink your theoretical framework.

When you come to the conclusion that your theories and operationalization are fine, it is usually a good idea to prefer the theoretical argumentation over the p-value of one statistical test, and keep the model as it is.

7.2 Random sampling

The second basic assumption is that your data is from a (simple) random sample, meaning that every unit of the population has the same (nonzero) chance of getting picked for the sample. This assumption is often violated when clustering occurs. For example, when you want to collect general information about the population of a country, it would be desirable to sample from a national register that contains every single person. As this is often not available, a common step is to first sample cities and then sample from a city-based register. This is convenient and brings the cost down, as interviewers only have to visit a limited number of places. The problem is that persons within one cluster are probably somewhat similar, and, therefore, units are not completely independent of each other. Consequently, the random sampling assumption is violated. Other examples are regions, nested within countries, or people nested within families. When you are confronted with this problem, using multilevel models is a solution (Rabe-Hesketh and Skrondal, 2012: 73–137). Another remedy is to control for the stage-two variable (for example, the city). Estimated effects are then independent of place of sampling.

7.3 Linearity in parameters

In a linear regression the relationship between your dependent and independent variables has to be linear. For illustration, say the coefficient of the variable total work experience is 2.5, which means, one more year of job experience results in an income that is increased by 2.5$. This effect has to be stable, no matter whether the change of your experience is from 2 to 3 years or from 20 to 21 years. In reality, we experience that this assumption is often violated, especially when dealing with the variable age, as saturation effects occur. When we think about the effect of age on wages, we would expect that, for young people there is a positive relationship, as people gain experience over time, that makes them more valuable. This relationship will get weaker as people reach their peak performance. When people get even older, their energy and speed will decline, due to biological effects of aging, therefore, wages will start to decline. It is obvious that the relationship between age and wages is not constant over time, but looks like a reversed U. Whenever this occurs, the regression will yield biased results, as it assumes strict linearity. For illustration, the following graph shows the actual connection between age and household income, taken from the German ALLBUS dataset (N=2,572):

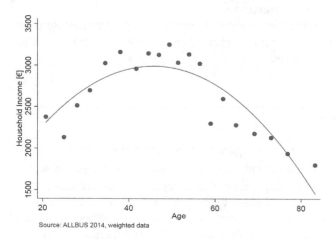

Source: ALLBUS 2014, weighted data

The first step is to check the relationship between the dependent variable and every independent variable graphically. Note that this only makes sense when the independent variable is metric, as binary (dummy) variables always have a linear relation to the dependent variable. A simple scatterplot gives you a first impression as to whether the relationship is linear or not.

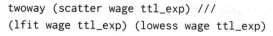

```
twoway (scatter wage ttl_exp) ///
(lfit wage ttl_exp) (lowess wage ttl_exp)
```

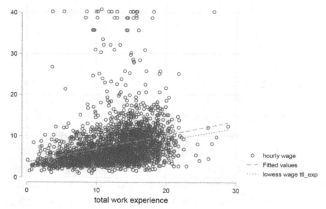

This command creates three plots in one image. The first part creates a simple scatterplot which we already know. The second part lets Stata fit a straight line through the data points, while the last command creates a locally weighted graph which can be different from a straight line. Luckily we come to the conclusion that the relation of our only metric variable and the dependent variable is fairly linear, as the linear fit and the lowess fit are very close to each other (apart from a small region to the right). This means that our assumption is probably fulfilled. You can also use the *binscatter* CCS, which I personally enjoy very much (see page 58).

Another option is to use residuals to check for nonlinearity. When you run a regression, Stata can save the predicted value for each case. As we want to explain wages through some other variables, Stata can calculate the wage that is predicted by the model, for each case. The difference between the observed value of wage, and the predicted value, is the residual. For example, when a respondent has a wage of 10 and the regression predicts a wage of 12, then the residual is -2 for this person. Usually you want the residuals to be as small as possible. When we plot residuals against our variables and cannot detect any pattern in the data points, the relation seems linear. For point-and-click go **Statistics -> Postestimation** and choose **Predictions -> Predictions and their SEs, leverage statistics, distance statistics, etc.**

```
regress wage c.ttl_exp i.union i.south c.grade
predict r1, residuals        //Create residuals
scatter r1 ttl_exp           //No pattern visible
```

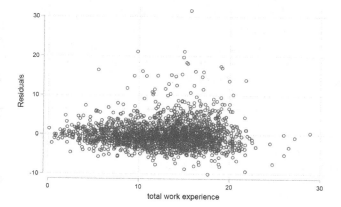

```
binscatter r1 ttl_exp          //Alternative command with CCS
```

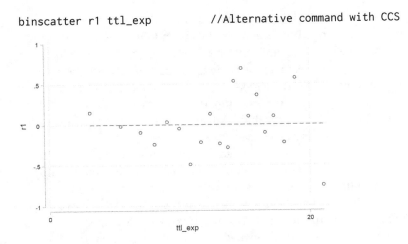

7.3.1 Solutions

When you come to the conclusion in your own analysis that a relation is not linear you can try to save your model by introducing higher ordered terms as additional variables in your model (polynomial regression). For example, let's say the variable age causes the problem. Then you can use Stata's factor variable notation (include the term *c.age##c.age* or even *c.age##c.age##c.age*, a three-way interaction).[2] How exactly you want to model and transform your independent variable depends on the functional form of the relationship with the dependent variable. After you had your command run you can use the calculated R-squared to assess the model fit. When the value went up this tells you that your new model is probably better.

If this still does not help you, take a look at the idea of a *piecewise regression*, or at the commands *gmm*, *nl* or *npregress kernel*[3] (warning: these are for experienced users and require a lot of understanding to yield valid results).

Nested models

Often you want to compare different models to find the variable transformation that helps you best to describe the distribution of your data points mathematically. R-squared is a statistic that is very commonly used to do this, as higher values indicate a better model fit. However, this is not without problems, especially when you want to compare nested models. A nested model is a subset of another model. For example, when you want to predict wage and use the variables south and union and after that, you run a second model which uses the variables south, union and work experience, then the first model is nested inside the second , as the explaining variables are a subset of the second model. By doing this you want to see which model is better to describe reality. The problem is that you usually

---

2 For an explanation see Wooldridge (2016): 173–177.
3 Introduced in version 15.

cannot compare R-squared values over nested models. Luckily other statistics can help you out. Akaikes Information Criterion (AIC) or the Bayesian Information Criterion (BIC) are suited to do this. You can get them by running your model and typing

```
estat ic
```

```
Akaike's information criterion and Bayesian information criterion
```

Model	Obs	ll(null)	ll(model)	df	AIC	BIC
.	1,876	-5340.121	-5008.277	5	10026.55	10054.24

```
Note: N=Obs used in calculating BIC; see [R] BIC note.
```

or click **Statistics → Postestimation → Reports and statistics.**

So run both models, calculate the AIC (or BIC) for both and compare which model has the *lower* value (lower means better here).

That brings up another important step in data handling: when you want to compare nested models you have to make sure that the number of cases used is identical and thus comparable. For example, your second model includes one additional variable but has missing values. Then, as Stata throws out cases that have even one missing on any variable used (listwise deletion), model two will use fewer cases than model one. When you get different results this can be due to the fact that the new variable has a significant effect but can also arise when you analyze a different subgroup (for example, you include income, but rich people do not want to answer this question and thus have missing values. Consequently, many rich people are excluded from the analysis, which might bias your results). To avoid this mistake check the model with the highest number of variables included and delete (or flag) all cases that have one or more missings on the variables used.

You can also use Stata internals to make this more convenient. You start with your complex model (the one with the highest number of independent variables), store the results and then run the simple model, using only cases that are already in the complex one:

```
regress DP IV1 IV2 IV3          //MComplex
estimates store complex         //Save results
regress DP IV1 if _est_complex  //MSimple
```

7.4 Multicollinearity

When you have a large number of independent (control) variables it can be problematic if there are strong correlations among these. For example, you could have one variable age, measured in years, and you create a second variable which measures age in months. This variable is the value of the first variable multiplied by 12. This is a problem for Stata, as both variables basically contain the same information and one of the two variables must be dropped from the analysis (to be more precise: one of the two is a linear combination of the other). Sometimes there is no perfect linear combination that predicts another variable but a strong correlation, maybe when you use two operationalizations of intelligence that have a high correlation. If this happens the standard errors of estimated coefficients can be inflated, which you want to avoid. You can test for multicollinearity after you run your model with the command

```
estat vif
```

Variable	VIF	1/VIF
ttl_exp	1.04	0.964467
1.union	1.03	0.970073
1.south	1.03	0.969747
grade	1.05	0.951913
Mean VIF	1.04	

or click **Statistics → Postestimation → Reports and statistics.**

VIF is the variance inflation factor. As a rule of thumb, any values above 10 are probably critical and should be investigated. When you include squared terms, as described in chapter 7.3.1 to account for nonlinear relations it is normal that the added terms have a high multicollinearity with the variables from which they are derived.

7.4.1 Solutions

When you notice that some variables have an unusually large value for VIF it could help to exclude one them from the regression and check whether the problem persists. Another variable probably already accounts for a large part of the aspect you try to measure, as correlation is high. Also you should think theoretically how the variables you used are related to each other and whether there are any connections. Maybe you can find another variable that has a lower correlation with the other explaining variables but can account for a part of your theory or operationalization.

7.5 Heteroscedasticity

Like explained above, after running your regression you can easily compute residuals, which are the differences between predicted and actual values for each case. One assumption of regressions is that the variance of these errors is identical for all values of the independent variables (Kohler and Kreuter, 2012: 296). Stated otherwise, the variance of the residuals has to be constant.[4] If this assumption is violated and the actual variance is not constant we call this heteroscedasticity.[5] We can check this by plotting residuals against predicted values

---

4 In mathematical notation: $Var\,(\epsilon_i) = \sigma^2$

5 Also see the introduction of Richard Williams (2015): https://www3.nd.edu/~rwilliam/stats2/l25.pdf (2018-02-10).

```
rvfplot, yline(0)
```

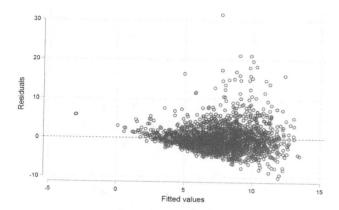

or click **Statistics → Linear models and related → Regression diagnostics → Residual-versus-fitted plot**. Each data point represents one observation. We see that there is a pattern in the data: to the left the points are all very close to the dotted line while the distance grows the further we move to the right. We see like a triangular distribution of the dots which clearly indicates that the variance is not homogeneous and, therefore, the assumption is violated. We can also test this assumption numerically by typing

```
estat hettest
```

```
Breusch-Pagan / Cook-Weisberg test for heteroskedasticity
        Ho: Constant variance
        Variables: fitted values of wage

        chi2(1)       =      191.93
        Prob > chi2   =      0.0000
```

or click **Statistics → Postestimation → Specification, diagnostic, and goodness-of-fit analysis** and choose **Tests for heteroscedasticity**, then click **Launch**. The null hypothesis is that there is a constant variance of the residuals. As the p-value (*Prob > chi2*) is smaller than 0.05, we have to reject this assumption. This further underlines that there is a violation.[6]

---

6 Here you see that "significant" not always means "good". Keep in mind that p-values can be used for a wide range of statistical hypothesis tests. The meaning of the result depends on how the hypotheses are formulated, which is arbitrary. Therefore, always pay attention to what your null- and alternative hypothesis state. In this case here, Stata is so nice and displays the null hypothesis as a reminder (*HO: Constant variance*).

7.5.1 Solutions

Heteroscedasticity often occurs when the distribution of the dependent variable is very skewed. It is a good idea to have a look at this, probably with a histogram

```
histogram wage                  //Graphic see page 51
```

This clearly shows that most values are between 0 and 15 and above that there are only a few cases left. There are many ways to solve this problem. What you should do depends on your goals. If you are only interested in interpreting signs and p-values (to see if there is any significant effect at all) you can transform the dependent variable and live with it. In contrast to that, when you want to make predictions and get more information out of the data, you will certainly need a re-transformation to yield interpretable values, which is a little more complex. Therefore, I will start with the simple solutions and proceed with a little more advanced options.

Signs and p-values

To receive trustable results with small standard errors when heteroscedasticity is present, it must be your goal to make the distribution of your dependent variable as symmetric and normal as possible. The idea is to apply a mathematical transformation to achieve this. The best way to start is often to check visually which transformation might be best. So type:

```
gladder wage
```

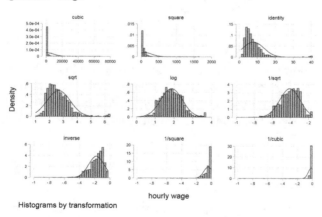

Histograms by transformation

or click **Statistics → Summaries, tables, and tests → Distributional plots and tests → Ladder of powers**. You will receive several histograms that depict how the variable looks after performing a transformation. Pick the one that looks most symmetrical and normally distributed, in our case the log-transformation.

```
generate lwage = log(wage)⁷
quietly regress lwage c.ttl_exp i.union i.south c.grade
estat hettest
```

```
Breusch-Pagan / Cook-Weisberg test for heteroskedasticity
        Ho: Constant variance
        Variables: fitted values of lwage

        chi2(1)      =      6.52
        Prob > chi2  =    0.0107
```

You will notice that the graphical distribution of the data points is much more equal and signals homogeneity. The numerical test is still significant, but the p-value is larger and thus we reduced the amount of the problem. If you think this is still not good enough, you can try the Box-Cox-transformation.

```
bcskew0 bcwage = wage
histogram bcwage
```

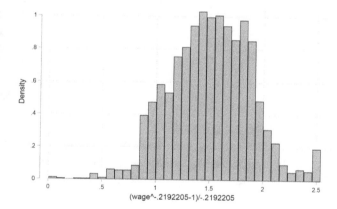

You find this command under **Data → Create or change data → Other variable-creation commands → Box-Cox transform**.

We conclude that this distribution is clearly more symmetrical than before. You can now run another regression with bcwage as the dependent variable and interpret

---

7 *Log()* or *Ln()* is the natural logarithm in Stata, so Euler's number is used as the base. If you want the logarithm with base 10, use *log10(wage)*.

the signs and p-values of the variables of interest. The problem of heteroscedasticity should be greatly reduced.

Predicted values

Often it is more important to actual predict values for certain constellations than to only conclude that a certain variable has a significant influence or not. If you need this, a little more work is required so you receive results that are accessible to non-statisticians. The first and super-easy option is run a normal regression model without any changes and specify robust standard errors. Stata will apply different algorithms that can deal better with heteroscedasticity.

```
regress wage c.ttl_exp i.union i.south c.grade, vce(robust)
```

```
Linear regression                               Number of obs   =       1,876
                                                F(4, 1871)      =      214.07
                                                Prob > F        =      0.0000
                                                R-squared       =      0.2980
                                                Root MSE        =      3.4975
```

wage	Coef.	Robust Std. Err.	t	P>|t|	[95% Conf. Interval]	
ttl_exp	.266036	.0164847	16.14	0.000	.2337057	.2983663
union						
union	.8229425	.2054872	4.00	0.000	.4199342	1.225951
1.south	-1.011447	.1673644	-6.04	0.000	-1.339687	-.6832065
grade	.5909214	.0367896	16.06	0.000	.5187684	.6630743
_cons	-3.392946	.4532821	-7.49	0.000	-4.281938	-2.503955

You will notice that the coefficients are identical to the normal regression, but the standard errors and, therefore, also the confidence intervals changed slightly. You can compare the results to the same model which uses regular standard errors (see page 92). To summarize it, you can use robust standard errors when you expect high heteroscedasticity but keep in mind that they are not magic and when your model is highly misspecified they will not save your results. Some statisticians recommend to calculate normal and robust standard errors and compare results: if the difference is large the model is probably poorly specified and should be revised carefully (King and Roberts, 2015). So you see, this option can be helpful in some cases, but sometimes it will not yield the best outcomes.

If you come to the conclusion that robust standard errors will not really improve your model, you can transform your dependent variable, as described above, and later re-transform the predictions to produce results that can be interpreted easily. We will choose a log-transformation for the example (make sure you have created the logged variable as explained before):

```
quietly regress lwage c.ttl_exp i.union i.south c.grade
margins union, at(ttl_exp=(0(4)24)) expression(exp(predict(xb)))
marginsplot
```

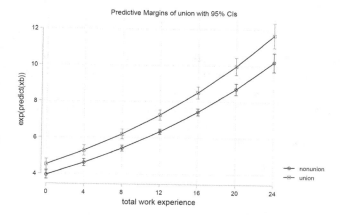

The magic happens in the option *expression*. We specify that the exponential-function (exp) should be applied to the result, as this is the inverse-function of the log-function. Finally, Stata produces a nice graph for us which shows the effect of union-membership for certain values of work experience. This method is not restricted to the log-function, as long as you specify the correct inverse-function for re-transformation. Note that this is an advanced topic and you should further research the literature, as the "best" transformation, or method, also depends on your research question and your variables. For example, some statisticians even prefer a poisson model over the regression with a log-transformed variable.[8]

7.6 Influential observations

Sometimes there are extraordinary cases in your dataset that can significantly influence results. It can be useful to find and investigate these cases in detail, as it might be better to delete them. This can be the case if they are extreme outliers, or display a very rare or special combination of properties (or just plain coding errors). To find these cases, Stata can compute different statistics.

---
8 https://blog.stata.com/2011/08/22/use-poisson-rather-than-regress-tell-a-friend/ (2018-07-22).

7.6.1 Dfbetas

The first option for checking special cases are Dfbetas. Run your regression model as usual and type

```
dfbeta
```

or click **Statistics → Linear models and related → Regression diagnostics → DFBETAs,** name the new variable and click **Submit.**

Stata creates four new variables (one for each metric or binary variable and one for each category of a categorical variable). You can get a nice visualization by typing

```
scatter _dfbeta_1 idcode, mlabel(idcode)
```

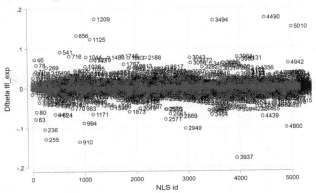

The further the absolute distance of a value from zero the greater the influence. You can check the cases which seem the most distant and inspect them individually. Then repeat for all other created dfbetas. There is a rule of thumb to estimate the value above which cases are problematic, which is calculated by the formula $\frac{2}{\sqrt{(n)}}$, where n is the number of cases (observations) used in the model. In our example this would be $\frac{2}{\sqrt{(1876)}} = 0.0462$

We can get a complete list of all cases that violate this limit by typing

```
list if abs(_dfbeta_1) > 0.0462 & !missing(_dfbeta_1)
count if abs(_dfbeta_1) > 0.0462 & !missing(_dfbeta_1)
```

- output omitted -

Do not forget to exclude cases with missing values, as otherwise these will be listed as well!

According to this, 83 cases are problematic (this is the result for the first dfbeta only). As there is no general rule for dealing with these cases, it is up to you to inspect and decide. When you do nothing and just ignore influential observations, it is also fine, as these are rarely discussed in research papers. When you are unsure what to do, consult your advisor (as he or she is the one who will grade your paper).

7.6.2 Cook's distance

When you do not like Dfbetas, since they are tedious to check when you use a great number of variables in your model, an alternative is Cook's distance which summarizes all information in just one variable. This measurement detects strange patterns and unusual variable constellations and can help to identify coding errors or problematic cases. As usual, run your model first and type

```
predict cook, cooksd
scatter cook idcode, mlabel(idcode)
```

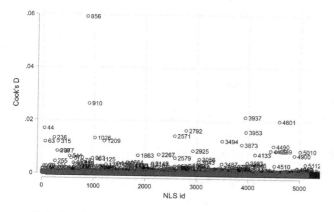

or click **Statistics → Linear models and related → Regression diagnostics → Cook's distance,** name the new variable and click **Submit.**

You can now inspect the scatterplot visually and have a look at the problematic cases that have unusually large values. One example is clearly case number 856, so we will list the relevant information for that particular observation.

```
list wage ttl_exp union south grade if idcode == 856
```

	wage	ttl_exp	union	south	grade
345.	39.23074	15.67308	union	1	12

This person has an extraordinarily high income, although her education is only medium and she is from the south. In general, this is a strange constellation which causes the high leverage of this case on the results.

A final possibility is to use leverage-versus-squared-residual plots which combine information about the leverage and residuals. This makes detection of outliers easy. Just run your regression and type

```
lvr2plot, mlabel(idcode)
```

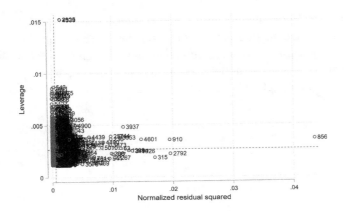

This plot shows for each case, the individual leverage (y-axis) and residual (x-axis). If the residual of a case is high, this tells us that our model makes a prediction that is quite off from the real outcome. Therefore, the residual is related to the dependent variable of the case. A high leverage of a case tells us that the constellations of independent variables of a certain case are so extreme, or uncommon, that they influence our final result over proportionally. Therefore, the leverage is related to the independent variables of a case. The two dotted lines in the graph show the means for both residuals and leverages. The diagnostics reported here are not exhaustive, as a much longer list of tests and method exists that can be used to assess the results of a regression. By listing the most important aspects that you should always control, I think that the results should be quite robust and suitable for publication. It is always a good idea to ask the people who will later receive your paper whether they have extra suggestions for tests that you should apply. Also, have a look at the literature and footnotes throughout the chapter, as they provide valuable information.

7.7 Summary

The following table (Table 7.1) will summarize the most important aspects we have learnt so far. Also keep in mind that bias is usually worse for your results than inflated standard errors.

Table 7.1: Summary of linear regression diagnostics.

Criterium	Exogeneity	Linearity	Multicollinearity	Heteroscedasticity	Influential Observations
Diagnostic	Theoretical Reasoning *estat ovtest*	*(bin)scatter DP IV* Scatterplots for the predicted values against each independent metric variable	*estat vif*	*rvfplot* *estat hettest*	*Dfbetas* Cook's Distance *lvr2plot*
Remedy	Include further important variables	Include higher ordered terms Do not use *linear* regression	Remove variables with values larger than 10	Transform dependent variable Use robust standard errors Retransformation	Remove influential observations or explain why you keep them
Effect of Violation	Biased Results	Biased Results	Inflated Standard Errors	Inflated Standard Errors	–

Macros

Sometimes it is necessary to run a command several times, with different options, to compare results, or to just play around with specifications. When you use a command which includes many variables, typing it all the time can get tiring. Another very common scenario is that you run a model with some control variables and later get feedback from your colleagues who suggest that you add some more variables. Now, you probably have to add these new variables at every place in your do-file, to update your code, which is error-prone.

A solution to this is to use local macros which allow you to define lists of variables at one place and then use them en block. When you come back later and want to add or delete variables, you only have to do so in one place. The general syntax is easy:

```
local controls c.age c.tenure i.race
regress wage i.union `controls'⁹
```

The first line defines the macro with they keyword *local*. After that you put the name ("controls"). Then a list of all variables follows, here with factor variable notation. The second line runs a regression with wage as a dependent variable. There will be four independent variables, union and the three others,

---

9 Note that the opening and closing symbols are different. The first character is the *grave accent*, the second one the *apostrophe*.

which are included in "controls". The macro must be typed in a do-file and only "lives" as long as the do-file is executed. After that you cannot use the local again, say, in the command line.

The counterpart to local macros is **global macros**. The main difference is that these macros can be used as often as you want, and they will still be in memory after your do-file has run. You can change a global macro anytime by redefining it. The usage is similar:

```
global test grade wage
summarize $test
```

To refer to the global macro the dollar-sign is used as a prefix. Keep in mind that globals can be problematic when it comes to debugging, as old or "forgotten" macros might haunt you later on.

8 Logistic regression*

Linear regressions can be used, as long as the dependent variable is metric (examples of metric variables are wage, working hours per week or blood pressure). We often encounter data that does not fit this metric, as it is binary. Classical examples are: whether somebody is pregnant, voted in the last elections or has died, as only two possibilities (states) exist. This chapter will shortly introduce logistic regressions which are used when these types of variables should be explained. As we will not talk about any statistical foundations of the method, you are advised to have a look at the literature, for a general introduction (Acock, 2014: 329–345; Long and Freese, 2014). It is also recommended that beginners read chapter six about linear regressions first before starting here. Finally I want to underline that I will only introduce predicted probabilities, as Odds Ratios or Logits seem no longer adequate in the presence of unobserved heterogeneity, and are especially hard to grasp for beginners.

8.1 Introduction

When running linear regressions we can explain the influence on a dependent metric variable in a fashion like "People who are union members earn on average 1.5 $ more per hour than other people." Pay attention to the metric of our prediction, which is measured in dollars, years, points or any other metric unit. When we deal with binary variables this is no longer possible, and we have to start thinking in probabilities. In a logistic regression, an independent variable can only influence the probability of going from one state (0) to the other (1).

In our example we want to research the effect of age on the chance of having a heart attack. The coding of the dependent variable is binary: people either had a heart attack or not, therefore, we use a logistic model. The independent variable is metric. Note that the arrow of causation can only point in one direction, as age can cause heart attacks, but heart attacks cannot cause (or influence) age. We will also introduce control variables, to account for spurious correlations.

To see the method in action, we will load another dataset which is taken from the second National Health and Nutrition Examination Survey (NHANES II)[1] which surveyed people in the USA about their health and diets between 1976 and 1980. We will use a sample of the data, which is not representative of the general population of the USA. Furthermore, we will ignore the sampling design, which introduces bias. Consequently, our results will not be valid in general or meet scientific standards,

---

[1] http://www.stata-press.com/data/r12/nhanes2.dta (2018-02-26).

https://doi.org/10.1515/9783110617160-008

yet will be adequate for the purpose of demonstrating the technique. We open the dataset by typing

```
webuse nhanes2, clear
```

First we inspect our dependent variable (heartatk) and our central independent variable (age), to get an impression of the general distribution of the data

```
tabulate heartatk
```

heart attack, 1=yes, 0=no	Freq.	Percent	Cum.
0	9,873	95.40	95.40
1	476	4.60	100.00
Total	10,349	100.00	

```
summarize age, detail
```

```
                          age in years
        Percentiles      Smallest
 1%         20               20
 5%         21               20
10%         24               20        Obs            10,351
25%         31               20        Sum of Wgt.    10,351

50%         49                         Mean           47.57965
                          Largest      Std. Dev.      17.21483
75%         63               74
90%         69               74        Variance       296.3503
95%         72               74        Skewness      -.1227378
99%         74               74        Kurtosis       1.561442
```

We see that about 4.6% of all respondents suffered a heart attack, and age ranges from 20 to 74 years, with an arithmetic mean of 47.6. Also have a look at the coding of the dependent variable, as 0 stands for "no attack" and 1 stands for "attack". The dependent variable must have exactly two numerical values, zero (0) and one (1). Stata will treat zero as the base category or "negative outcome". Other coding schemes are not accepted.[2] To see whether any association between the two variables exists, we can use Spearman's Rho (see page 67):

---

2 Type *set showbaselevels on, perm* so Stata always display the category of reference.

```
spearman heartatk age
```

```
 Number of obs =    10349
Spearman's rho =       0.2037
```

```
Test of Ho: heartatk and age are independent
     Prob > |t| =       0.0000
```

The result underlines that there is a positive association, which is highly significant (Prob > |t| is smaller than 0.05). This result will not surprise us, as we know in general that older people have more heart attacks, due to the biological consequences of aging on blood vessels.

Why can't we just use a linear regression to calculate the results? The main problem is that the model is probably not linear at all. This means that the probability of suffering a heart attack is not constant over the years, but further increases with age. The effect of an increase of one year will only slightly increase the probability of having a heart attack when you are 25, but much higher when you are 75, therefore, we have nonlinearity in the parameters. We will now test this empirically by running the logistic regression, with age as the only predictor. We also use the factor variable notation, as in chapter six, where continuous variables receive the prefix c. and binary and ordinal variables receive the prefix i.

```
logit heartatk c.age          //M1
```

```
Iteration 0:    log likelihood = -1930.5936
Iteration 1:    log likelihood = -1725.2051
Iteration 2:    log likelihood = -1670.5994
Iteration 3:    log likelihood = -1669.2695
Iteration 4:    log likelihood = -1669.2671
Iteration 5:    log likelihood = -1669.2671
```

```
Logistic regression                          Number of obs   =      10,349
                                             LR chi2(1)      =      522.65
                                             Prob > chi2     =      0.0000
Log likelihood = -1669.2671                  Pseudo R2       =      0.1354
```

heartatk	Coef.	Std. Err.	z	P>|z|	[95% Conf. Interval]	
age	.0841126	.004814	17.47	0.000	.0746773	.0935478
_cons	-7.806905	.3079539	-25.35	0.000	-8.410484	-7.203326

When you want to use point-and-click, go **Statistics → Binary Outcomes → Logistic Regression**, enter heartatk under "Dependent variable" and age under "Independent variables", then click **Submit**.

The output is similar to that of a linear regression. Pseudo R2 estimates the variance that can be explained using the model, which is about 13.5%. We see that the coefficient for age is positive (0.084) and highly significant (p-value smaller than 0.01). The problem is that, due to the nonlinear character of the model, we can only interpret the *sign* of the coefficient. Although this might seem disappointing, statisticians have shown that any other interpretation can be highly biased (Mood, 2010). This means that an increased age will result in an increased probability of having a heart attack (the higher the age, the higher the probability). As Stata uses 0 as the point of reference ("no event"), the change to the other category (1, "event") is explained in the model. If the coding was reversed we would receive a negative coefficient for age.

We also want to see the nonlinear character of the predicted probabilities that was assumed by the theoretical argumentation. To assess this, we can calculate predicted values. Based on the model, Stata will estimate the probability for each person of suffering a heart attack.

```
predict predi        //Predict estimated probabilities
scatter predi age    //Scatterplot
```

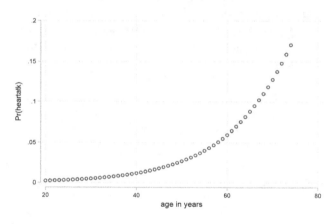

The scatterplot shows the nonlinear relation, as the slope increases with age.

To receive more concrete results, we can calculate predicted probabilities using the *margins* command:

```
margins
```

```
Predictive margins                        Number of obs    =     10,349
Model VCE    : OIM

Expression   : Pr(heartatk), predict()
```

	Margin	Delta-method Std. Err.	z	P>|z|	[95% Conf. Interval]
_cons	.0459948	.002006	22.93	0.000	.0420632 .0499264

When you want to use point-and-click, go **Statistics** → **Postestimation** → **Marginal means and predictive margins**, click "At" and select **All covariates at their means in the sample**, then click **Submit**.

It is worth taking some time to understand what is happening here. Stata reports a single number (0.046) that is the average probability for someone from our sample of suffering a heart attack. What Stata does is the following: the coefficients from the logit model above are used to separately calculate the predicted chance of having an event for every person. Then Stata reports the arithmetic mean of these predicted probabilities. To see that this is true, we can do it ourselves. As we have saved the predicted probability already in the variable predi, we can summarize it by typing

summarize predi

Variable	Obs	Mean	Std. Dev.	Min	Max
predi	10,351	.0459878	.0472867	.0021835	.170431

You see that the result is 0.046 as well. Note that standard errors are different, as *margins* is more complex and calculates other statistics (as confidence intervals) as well. A second option is the marginal outcome at the mean:

margins, atmeans

| Adjusted predictions | | | | Number of obs | = | 10,349 |
Model VCE   : OIM

Expression : Pr(heartatk), predict()
at   : age   =   47.5818 (mean)

	Margin	Delta-method Std. Err.	z	P>|z|	[95% Conf. Interval]
_cons	.0217814	.0019011	11.46	0.000	.0180552	.0255075

What happens here is different from the first *margins* command. Now Stata calculates the empiric arithmetic mean for every independent variable in the model (in this case only for age, that is 47.6 years) and internally changes the age of every person to this value. Then it predicts individual probabilities and averages the result. You see that the outcome (0.02) is not equal to the first one (0.046). Here we learn that a person who is 47.6 years old, has a probability of 2.2% of suffering a heart attack on average. You have to decide theoretically which result you want. You see that this decision is important, as outcomes might differ largely!

We can extend this logic, and produce more informative graphs by not calculating just one single prediction at the mean, but for a wide range of ages. The next command will calculate the probability for every single age from 20 to 74 and then make a pretty graph out of it.

```
quietly margins, at(age=(20(1)74))
marginsplot, recast(line) recastci(rarea)
```

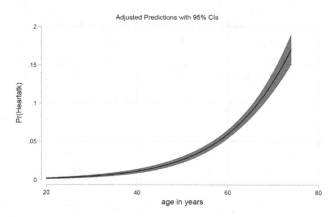

To create the graph using point-and-click, go **Statistics → Postestimation → Margins plots and profile plots**. To change the look of the line and confidence intervals click "Plot" and "CI plot" and test out the variety of options, then click **Submit**.

The options used with *marginsplot* make our graph somewhat elegant and more informative. Now we can easily read the probability by age of someone having a heart attack, which also includes a 95% confidence interval. Again we see the inherent non-linear character of the model: the probability is almost constant between 30 and 40 years, but quite steep between 60 and 70 years. Although both intervals have the same length, the increase in probability of having a heart attack is quite different.

Finally, we can also calculate Average Marginal Effects (AMEs), which are the preferred option when it comes to reporting results for nonlinear models.

```
margins, dydx(age)                //Calculate AMEs for age
```

```
Average marginal effects                   Number of obs     =      10,349
Model VCE     : OIM

Expression    : Pr(heartatk), predict()
dy/dx w.r.t.  : age
```

	dy/dx	Delta-method Std. Err.	z	P>|z|	[95% Conf. Interval]
age	.0035027	.0002319	15.10	0.000	.0030482 .0039573

or click **Statistics** → **Postestimation** → **Marginal Effects** and enter age under "Variables:". Make sure that **Marginal effects of response** and **Marginal effects d(y)/d(x)** are both ticked, then click **Submit**.

The result is 0.00350, which tell us that, on average, an increase of age of one year will increase the probability of suffering a heart attack by 0.35 percentage points (not percent!). This interpretation is favored by econometricians, yet is often not really intuitive when we talk about continuous variables like age.[3] We will later see how an interpretation with categorical variables is more natural. As a side note: if dydx rings a bell, it is because Stata calculates the derivative of the equation, estimated in the logit command, with respect to age. The result is the slope of the graph, which is the instantaneous rate of change.

8.2 Control variables

Until now, we have only included age as an explanatory variable in the model, which is usually not a good idea, as other variables might help explaining the real relationship. Therefore, we want to add control variables, just as we did in the linear regression. On a theoretical base we decide that gender, Body-Mass-Index (BMI) and the region where a person lives, might be relevant factors, so we include them. Furthermore, as

```
Logistic regression                              Number of obs   =      10,349
                                                 LR chi2(7)      =      653.05
                                                 Prob > chi2     =      0.0000
Log likelihood =  -1604.069                      Pseudo R2       =      0.1691
```

heartatk	Coef.	Std. Err.	z	P>|z|	[95% Conf. Interval]	
age	.3444993	.0549643	6.27	0.000	.2367713	.4522273
c.age#c.age	-.0023064	.0004712	-4.89	0.000	-.0032299	-.0013829
bmi	.0208818	.0102486	2.04	0.042	.0007949	.0409687
region						
MW	.2781317	.1529419	1.82	0.069	-.021629	.5778924
S	.2603698	.1505407	1.73	0.084	-.0346844	.5554241
W	.4546817	.1481829	3.07	0.002	.1642485	.7451148
sex						
Female	-.9184638	.1025228	-8.96	0.000	-1.119405	-.7175229
_cons	-15.28402	1.610716	-9.49	0.000	-18.44096	-12.12707

---

3 A technical introduction can be found here: https://www3.nd.edu/~rwilliam/stats3/Margins02.pdf (2018–02-21).

we have already in the linear regression, we will include a higher ordered term for age. One might wonder why this is still relevant, as we talk about nonlinear effects anyway, but linearity between the logarithmic odds of the dependent variable, and all metric independent variables is still required (Kohler and Kreuter, 2012: 368). Our second model looks like this:

```
logit heartatk c.age##c.age c.bmi i.region i.sex      //M2
```

Due to the higher ordered term, it is quite impossible to interpret this model using coefficients, so we first compute Average Marginal Effects and then produce graphs.

```
margins, dydx(*)
```

```
Average marginal effects                    Number of obs    =    10,349
Model VCE      : OIM

Expression     : Pr(heartatk), predict()
dy/dx w.r.t.   : age bmi 2.region 3.region 4.region 2.sex
```

	dy/dx	Delta-method Std. Err.	z	P>|z|	[95% Conf. Interval]	
age	.002151	.0002937	7.32	0.000	.0015753	.0027268
bmi	.000859	.0004223	2.03	0.042	.0000313	.0016866
region						
MW	.010322	.0055944	1.85	0.065	-.0006429	.0212868
S	.0095908	.0054432	1.76	0.078	-.0010777	.0202593
W	.0181733	.0057527	3.16	0.002	.0068982	.0294483
sex						
Female	-.037319	.0041182	-9.06	0.000	-.0453905	-.0292475

Note: dy/dx for factor levels is the discrete change from the base level.

The asterisk means that the effects are computed for all variables in the model. We see that the AME for age was slightly reduced, yet is still highly significant. Quite interestingly gender accounts for a lot. The interpretation is as follows: women have on average (all other variables held constant) 3.7 percentage points lower probability of suffering a heart attack than men. The effect is highly significant.

To understand the AME as a counterfactual, we could ask: what would the probability be for an event, if every person in the sample was male? So Stata internally sets gender to male for all persons (men and women!), leaves the other covariates untouched, predicts the individual probabilities and averages them. Then it repeats the process, this time setting the gender to female, computing again the average probabilities and reporting the difference between the two averaged predictions, which is the AME.

To continue, we produce more detailed graphs which will also show the effect of age:

```
quietly margins, at(age=(20(1)74))
marginsplot, recast(line) recastci(rarea)
```

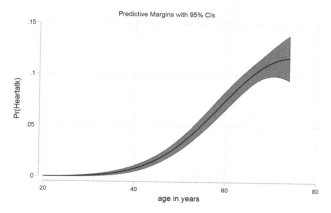

The results are quite similar to what we have seen before. We can now try to calculate separate effects for genders:

```
quietly margins sex, at(age=(20(1)74))
marginsplot, recast(line) recastci(rarea)
```

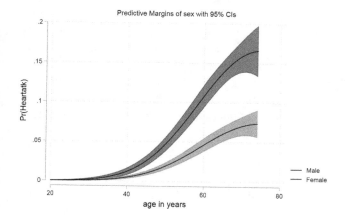

The results are impressive, and highlight the stark differences between men and women. Up to 40, the probabilities of having a heart attack are quite similar for men and women, after that the gap widens drastically. Note that we did not even have to specify an explicit interaction effect between age and gender, as this happens "automatically" in a logistic regression, as all variables are somehow related to each other.

Another option is to calculate Average Marginal Effects for gender, not only for the general model, but for a wider range of values for age.

```
quietly margins, dydx(sex) at(age=(20(1)74))
marginsplot, recast(line) recastci(rarea)
```

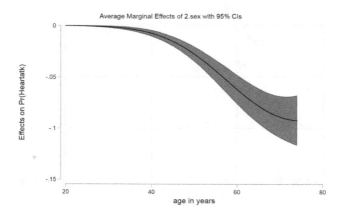

Remember that the AME tells you the marginal effect of changing gender, on the probability of having a heart attack. For example, in the graph above we see women with age 60 have a six percentage points lower probability of having a heart attack than men. We come to this conclusion, as the AME above is calculated for the 2.sex (see the title of the graph). As men are coded with zero and are, therefore, the category of reference, women are the second category, so the depicted effect shows the change from reference to this category. Additionally, a 95% confidence interval is included in the graph to improve the accuracy of your estimation.

One last option you can try is Marginal Effects at the Mean (MEM), which is just a combination of the aspects we have learned so far:

```
margins, dydx(sex) atmeans
```

The outcome tells us that when you had two otherwise-average individuals, one male, one female, the probability of having a heart attack would be 2.1 percentage points lower for the female.

```
Conditional marginal effects                   Number of obs    =    10,349
Model VCE     : OIM

Expression    : Pr(heartatk), predict()
dy/dx w.r.t.  : 2.sex
at            : age          =      47.5818 (mean)
                bmi          =     25.53789 (mean)
                1.region     =      .202435 (mean)
                2.region     =     .2679486 (mean)
                3.region     =     .2756788 (mean)
                4.region     =     .2539376 (mean)
                1.sex        =     .4749251 (mean)
                2.sex        =     .5250749 (mean)
```

	dy/dx	Delta-method Std. Err.	z	P>|z|	[95% Conf. Interval]	
sex						
Female	-.0206905	.0029562	-7.00	0.000	-.0264845	-.0148965

```
Note: dy/dx for factor levels is the discrete change from the base level.
```

8.3 Nested Models

What was explained on page 106 is also valid for logistic regressions: when you want to compare nested models make sure that they all use the same number of cases. You can use the AIC or the BIC to compare model fit (remember, lower values indicate better fitting models). Another option is the Likelihood-Ratio test, to see whether one model performs better than the other. To do this, estimate both models, save the results and run the test:

```
quietly logit heartatk c.age##c.age c.bmi i.region i.sex  //Run Model 1
estimates store Mfull                                      //Store results
quietly logit heartatk c.age if _est_Mfull                 //Run Model 2
estimate store Msimple                                     //Store results
lrtest Mfull Msimple
```

```
Likelihood-ratio test                      LR chi2(6)   =    130.40
(Assumption: Msimple nested in Mfull)      Prob > chi2  =    0.0000
```

When you want to use point-and-click, go **Statistics → Postestimation → Tests → Likelihood-ratio test**.

When you receive a significant result, you can conclude that the extended model (the one with the largest number of variables) has a better model fit than the nested model.

Note that the order of the models in the *lrtest* command is not important, as Stata automatically recognizes which model is the one with the fewer variables used. Also keep in mind that you can use Average Marginal Effects to compare effects across models or samples, which is not possible with Odds or Logits (Mood, 2010).

8.4 Diagnostics

A review of the literature shows that there is no clear consensus about the diagnostics that are relevant for logistic regressions for yielding valid results. The following section is an overview of some aspects that will contribute to your model quality. The good news is that logistic regressions have lower standards than linear ones, so violations might not have too severe consequences. We will use the following model for all diagnostics shown here:

```
logit heartatk c.age##c.age c.bmi i.region i.sex
```

8.4.1 Model misspecification

You should create a model based upon your theoretical considerations. You can, statistically, further test whether your model has any missing or unnecessary variables included. To do so, run your model and type

```
linktest
```

heartatk	Coef.	Std. Err.	z	P>|z|	[95% Conf. Interval]	
_hat	1.080761	.2095741	5.16	0.000	.6700029	1.491518
_hatsq	.0126761	.0311796	0.41	0.684	-.0484349	.0737871
_cons	.1117096	.3167557	0.35	0.724	-.5091202	.7325395

or click **Statistics → Postestimation → Tests → Specification link test for single-equation models**.

Stata produces a regression like output, with two variables, _hat and _hatsq. As long as the p-value of _hat is significant (p-value smaller than 0.05) and _hatsq is *not* significant (p-value larger than 0.05) your model specification should be fine. When _hat is not significant, your model is probably quite misspecified. When _hatsq is significant that means there are probably some important variables missing in your model. As you can see, our model should be OK.

8.4.2 Sample size and empty cells

Logistic models usually need more observations than linear regressions. Make sure to use at least 100 cases. When you have a lower number of cases, you can run an exact logistic regression (type *help exlogistic* for more information). Furthermore, it is vital that there are no empty cells in your model, which means that for any combination of your variables, there must be cases available. In the example above, we include the region (four categories) and the gender (two categories) as predictors, so there are eight cells (considering only these two variables). An empty cell is an interaction of levels of two or more factor variables for which there is no data available. When this happens, Stata will drop the respective categories automatically and not show them in the output. Having enough cases, in general, will reduce the chances that you have any empty cells.

8.4.3 Multicollinearity

Just like linear regressions, logistic ones are also influenced by a high correlation of independent variables. Testing this requires another user-written command (*collin*). Try

```
search collin
```

```
collin from https://stats.idre.ucla.edu/stat/stata/ado/analysis
    collin. Collinearity Diagnostics / Philip B. Ender / Statistical Computing
    and Consulting / UCLA Office of Academic Computing / ender@ucla.edu /
    STATA ado and hlp files in the package / distribution-date: 20101123


6 references found in tables of contents
----------------------------------------
```

Figure 8.1: The package collin in the online archive.

And look for the entry in the window that pops up (Figure 8.1). When the installation is complete, enter the command and the variables you used in the model:

```
collin age bmi region sex
```

```
  Collinearity Diagnostics
```

Variable	VIF	SQRT VIF	Tolerance	R-Squared
age	1.03	1.02	0.9704	0.0296
bmi	1.03	1.02	0.9706	0.0294
region	1.00	1.00	0.9997	0.0003
sex	1.00	1.00	0.9999	0.0001
Mean VIF	1.02			

	Eigenval	Cond Index
1	4.6862	1.0000
2	0.1370	5.8479
3	0.1051	6.6771
4	0.0567	9.0933
5	0.0150	17.6658

```
Condition Number          17.6658
Eigenvalues & Cond Index computed from scaled raw sscp (w/ intercept)
Det(correlation matrix)     0.9703
```

As a general rule of thumb it might be a good idea to readjust your model when a variable shows a VIF above 10. In this case, remove one variable with a high VIF and run your model again. If the VIF is lower for the remaining variables, the choice might be a good idea.

8.4.4 Influential observations

Some observations might have uncommon constellations for values in their variables, which makes them influence results over-proportionally. It is usually a good idea to inspect these cases, although there is no general rule on how to deal with them. When you can exclude the possibility of plain coding errors, you can either keep or drop these cases. In contrast to the linear regression, we will use a slightly different measurement for influential observations in logistic regressions (Pregibon's Beta, which is similar to Cook's Distance). After your model was run type

```
predict beta, dbeta
```

or click **Statistics → Postestimation → Predictions, residuals, etc.** and select **Delta-Beta influence statistic** and give a name to the newly created variable, then click **Submit.** You will notice that only one variable was created, which we will inspect now. The total leverage of each case is summarized in this one. To detect outliers, use a scatterplot to assess the general distribution of the variable and scrutinize the problematic cases.

```
scatter beta sampl, mlabel(sampl)
```

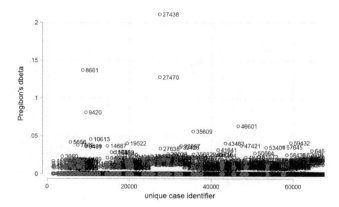

We see a few extreme outliers, for example case 27,438. What is wrong here? Let's have a closer look. We want to list all relevant values for this case, so we type

```
list heartatk sex age bmi region if sampl == 27438
```

	heartatk	sex	age	bmi	region
6879.	1	Female	28	27.40053	NE

The information here is perplexing. This woman with an age of 28 and a BMI of 27 (which counts as slightly overweight) reported a heart attack. Our common sense tells us that this is exceptional, as usually older men who are obese are prone to heart attacks. As this special case clearly violates the normal pattern, we could delete it and argue that this abnormal case influences our general results over-proportionally. Whatever you decide to do, report it in your paper and give a theoretical justification, as there is no general rule.

After you have excluded the case, run your model again and assess how the output changed.

```
logit heartatk c.age##c.age c.bmi i.region i.sex if sampl != 27438
```

- output omitted -

9 Matching

The last technique I want to introduce is propensity score matching (PSM).[1] What sounds fancy is often not included in the basic Stata textbooks, and actually quite easy to understand and interpret, even for the beginner. The next section will shortly discuss the main ideas behind the method, run an example and check some diagnostics afterwards.

9.1 Simulating an experiment

Experiments are regarded as the gold standard in science. Most people will know about experiments from the medical sciences, when new drugs are tested and one group receives the actual drug and the other one a placebo to assess the "real" effect of the new active component. What is the core of experiments? The answer is randomization. People that are sampled from a larger population are randomly assigned to two groups, the treatment group and the control. This guarantees that, on average, both groups are similar, with respect to visible (e.g. age, gender) and hidden (e.g. intelligence, motivation, health) properties. When the treatment (drug) is applied to one group and randomization was performed, we can be sure that any effect that happens is solely due to the treatment, as no other factors can influence the result. Basically, we could do this in the social sciences as well.[2] Suppose, we want to research the effect of education on success in life. We sample pupils from the population and randomly put some of them in elite schools, while others have to go to not so fancy schools. After some years, we see how the pupils are doing. As factors like intelligence, motivation or social and financial background were similar at the start of the experiment (due to the randomization) the differences later in life, between the groups, can be traced back to the effect of school alone. As you may expect, especially parents from wealthy families might not be happy when their child is randomly put in a low-quality school, which clearly underlines the ethical and economic problems of social experiments.

The idea of matching is to simulate an experiment, even when only observational data is available. Basically, the method tries to find pairs in the data which are similar in visible characteristics, and only differ in the treatment status. For example, when we find two girls that have the same age, intelligence and social background, but one of them went to the elite school while the other did not, then

---

1 For a general introduction to the method see the excellent overview of Caliendo and Kopeinig (2008). Note that some recommendations given there are already outdated. Recent information can be found here: https://www.stata.com/meeting/germany17/slides/Germany17_Jann.pdf (2018-02-02).
2 For an introduction see Shadish et al. (2002).

https://doi.org/10.1515/9783110617160-009

we have a matched pair. The basic problems of the method are the same as with regressions: only measured characteristics can be used as "controls" and matching is not a magic trick that introduces new information. The main advantages, in contrast to a regression are that the functional form of the relationship between treatment and outcome is not needed to be specified (so the problem of "linearity" we discussed before is gone) and the method is very close to the ideas of the counterfactual framework.

9.2 Propensity score matching

One problem in matching is that it is very hard or even impossible to find good matches when we use a lot of control variables. When we match on age, gender, education, intelligence, parental background, etc... it will be hard to find "statistical twins" in the data that have the exact same properties in all these variables. This is called the curse of dimensionality, which can be solved using propensity scores. The basic idea is to run a logistic regression which uses all control variables as independent variables, predict the chance of being in the treatment group, and then match using the score alone (which is a single number). The assumption is that people with a similar score will have similar properties. This has been proven mathematically, but still has some problems that were discussed recently (King and Nielsen, 2016). Therefore, we will rely on kernel-matching, which seems quite robust against some problems that are associated with matching. Based upon recent developments, I recommend this approach (possibly in combination with exact matching) over algorithms like nearest-neighbor or caliper.[3]

The problem is that Stata does not support kernel-matching, therefore, we will use a new command developed by Jann (2017) which implements a robust and fast version and comes with a lot of diagnostic options.

```
ssc install kmatch, replace              //Install CCS
```

Using this, we want to test the effect of being in a union on wage. As in chapter six, we will rely on NLSW88 data. Note that our dependent variable can be metric (continuous) or binary, and our treatment variable must be binary, so exactly two groups can be defined (treatment and control).[4] The independent variables can have any metric, as long as you use factor-variable notation. For the example, we choose total work

---

3 Stata comes with matching since version 13. Popular community-contributed commands are psmatch2 (*ssc install psmatch2*) and pscore (*ssc install st0026_2*).
4 If you want to compare several groups, for example more than one treatment drug, it is recommended to form all binary contrasts and run one matching model for each.

experience, region, age and smsa (metropolitan region) as control variables. Let's see this in action. We open our dataset and run the command:

```
sysuse nlsw88, clear
kmatch ps union c.ttl_exp i.south c.age i.smsa (wage)
```

```
Propensity-score kernel matching              Number of obs    =      1,878
                                              Kernel           =       epan
Treatment : union = 1
Covariates: ttl_exp i.south age i.smsa
PS model  : logit (pr)
```

Matching statistics

	Matched			Controls			Band-
	Yes	No	Total	Used	Unused	Total	width
Treated	441	20	461	998	419	1417	.00035
Untreated	1340	77	1417	457	4	461	.0011
Combined	1781	97	1878	1455	423	1878	.

Treatment-effects estimation

wage	Coef.
ATE	.9151725

The explanation is as follows: *kmatch* is the name of the command we want to use, *ps* tells Stata to perform propensity score matching. Union is the treatment variable (coded 0/1), followed by four (rather randomly chosen) control variables. Just as with regressions, you enter your variables with factor-variable notation. When desired, you can also include interactions or higher-ordered terms. The outcome variable (wage) is put in parentheses at the end of the command. Note that you can also include multiple outcomes in the same model.

The ATE (0.915), is displayed as a result, which is the Average Treatment Effect. This is the estimated difference between the means of the treatment, and control group for the outcome variable (wage). As we see that the value is positive, we know that the average effect of being in a union results in a plus on wage of about 92 cents per hour.

Now we would like to know whether this result is statistically significant. In contrast to a regression, p-values cannot be calculated in the regular way, but must be estimated, using bootstrapping (which is a form of resampling). On modern computers it is reasonable to use about 500 replications for bootstrapping (the larger the number, the less variable the results). To get these we type

```
kmatch ps union c.ttl_exp i.south c.age i.smsa (wage), ///
    vce(bootstrap, reps(500))
```

Treatment-effects estimation

wage	Observed Coef.	Bootstrap Std. Err.	z	P>|z|	Normal-based [95% Conf. Interval]	
ATE	.9151725	.2307688	3.97	0.000	.4628739	1.367471

This might take a few minutes to run , as a random sample is drawn 500 times and then the command is repeated for each. The result shows that the p-level is below 0.05 and,therefore the effect is statistically significant. Note that your results will probably differ from the one shown here, as resampling is based on random samples, thus the p-level and standard error will slightly deviate.[5]

When you are not interested in the ATE, you can also see the ATT (Average Treatment Effect on the Treated). This statistic tells us what people who are actually in a union earn more, due to the union membership. The counterpart is the ATC (Average Treatment Effect on the Control) which tells us how much more, people (who are not in a union) would earn, if they were union members. To get these effects add the options *att* or *atc*.

Finally, it seems like a good idea to combine PSM with an exact matching on certain key variables (here we choose college education). In other words, before the matching is run, Stata will match perfectly, which means that people with college education will be compared only to other people with the same level of education. The downside is that when you match on a large number of exact variables, the number of cases used will be lower, as a perfect match cannot always be found. It is usually a good idea to include only a few binary or ordinal variables for exact matching. Note that you cannot use factor variable notation or interactions in this option.

```
kmatch ps union c.ttl_exp i.south c.age i.smsa (wage), ///
    vce(bootstrap, reps(500)) att ematch(collgrad)
```

- Output omitted -

The option *att* tells Stata to report the ATT instead of the ATE, and *ematch(collgrad)* will combine the PSM with an exact matching on the variable collgrad. It is usually a good idea to, later, report the ATT, and the ATE, as these are often the most interesting results.

---

5 If you want your results to be replicable, use the command *set seed 1234* at the top of your do-file, where you replace 1234 with a "random" number of your choice. Furthermore, make sure to sort your cases by ID as random resorting could also influence the results (*sort idcode*).

9.3 Matching diagnostics

In contrast to linear regressions, matching has lower demands, which makes our lives easier, yet there are two central aspects that must be checked, to see if we can trust our results (the following diagnostics refer to the model from page 135).

9.3.1 Common support

As described above, when you run a PSM, Stata will start with a logit model to calculate (for each person) the propensity score that summarizes the probability of being in the treatment group. If some variables have perfect predictability, which means they flawlessly determine if a person is either in treatment or control, PSM will not work. For example, suppose that every person from the south is in the treatment group, and persons from other regions are in the control group. Then, the variable south perfectly predicts the treatment status, which is not allowed. Stated otherwise: when you divide the entire range of calculated propensity scores into an arbitrary number of groups, you need, within each group, both people from treatment and control. This can be visualized.

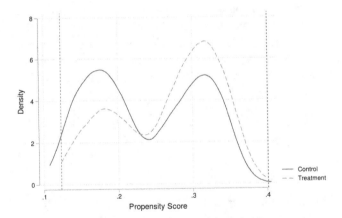

The region between the two vertical bars is the region of common support. Although *kmatch* automatically trims away cases outside that region (for example the people depicted by the continuous black graph to the very left), you still have to inspect this, as there might be other problems. Sometimes, there are regions in the middle of the spectrum, with very low values for one group, which can be problematic. Checking this will tell you how well the common support is fulfilled. In our case it looks fine. You can create this kind of graph automatically by typing

```
kmatch density            //Output omitted
```

Another important aspect to consider, are the cases that could not be matched. Almost always, there will be cases in your sample for which an adequate match could not be found, therefore, these cases will not be used for calculating the statistic of interest (for example the ATE). This means, your overall sample and the sample used to calculate the statistic differ, which might leads to bias. To check if this is a problem type

```
kmatch cdensity
```

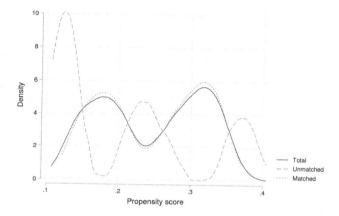

You see that the graphs of the "Total" sample and the "Matched" sample are very close to each other, meaning that the sample that could be used in the matching is almost identical to the overall sample on average. As long as this is the case, we do not expect any bias.

9.3.2 Balancing of covariates

Remember that a PSM tries to make two groups similar, that were quite different before the match, with respect to all independent variables in the model. It is a good idea to check whether this goal was actually achieved. The idea is simple: you inspect the means of these variables, within both groups, after the matching was done, and see if they are similar. As long as this is the case, you can be optimistic that your matching was successful. You can do this using either tables or graphs. We first start with a simple table.

```
kmatch summarize
```

You see that the standardized differences (mean) for total work experience was 0.13 before matching, and 0.02 after matching. This seems like a good result, also for the other variables. Keep in mind that the matched value should approach zero for means

Means	Raw			Matched(ATE)		
	Treated	Untrea~d	StdDif	Treated	Untrea~d	StdDif
ttl_exp	13.2539	12.6767	.125897	12.9591	12.8603	.021547
1.south	.295011	.46789	-.361431	.422557	.418636	.008199
age	39.2842	39.2054	.026	39.1406	39.2015	-.0201
1.smsa	.770065	.687368	.186677	.732999	.731973	.002316

Variances	Raw			Matched(ATE)		
	Treated	Untrea~d	Ratio	Treated	Untrea~d	Ratio
ttl_exp	20.7346	21.3093	.973031	17.8685	20.078	.889958
1.south	.208432	.249145	.836588	.24414	.243517	1.00256
age	9.13429	9.23816	.988756	9.07008	9.04185	1.00312
1.smsa	.17745	.215045	.825175	.195821	.196299	.997568

and one for the ratios of the standard deviations, which are listed below. All in all these results are very positive. If you prefer graphs over tables type

```
kmatch density ttl_exp south age smsa
```

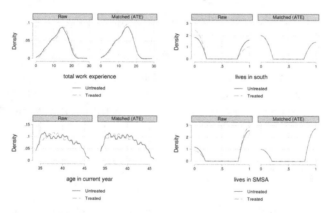

You see a plot comparing the distribution of each variable before and after the matching. The closer the two graphs resemble each other, after the matching, the better the balancing.

Finally, you can use Rosenbaum-Bounds to assess how robust your results are, with respect to omitted variables. This slightly advanced technique cannot be introduced here (check out the online resources), but is available using community-contributed software (Rosenbaum, 2002; Becker and Caliendo, 2007; DiPrete and Gangl, 2004).[6] To learn how this technique can be integrated in a research paper, refer to Gebel (2009).

---

6 Available user-written commands are *rbounds* (metric outcome variable) and *mhbounds* (binary outcome variable).

10 Reporting results

After you have finished the difficult part, and produced and tested your results, it is time to publish them. Usually this works fairly well, yet some things should be considered in order to reach a professional appearance. It is never a good idea to copy and past Stata output directly into a paper, as it will probably lower your grade. The first problem is that Stata produces a great amount of information that is often not needed in publications, as tables are already large enough and researchers don't have time to deal with every bit of information. The second aspect is that the Stata format is usually not what editors or professors expect when they think of a nice layout. It is always a good idea to study the most important journals of your field, to get an impression of what a table looks like there, so you can try to adopt this style in your own paper. Otherwise, ask your advisor for examples. We will use a quite generic formatting that could probably be used in any modern journal. We will use the results of the linear regression models from chapter six to produce tables and output.

10.1 Tables

Tables are at the heart of scientific research, as they compress a lot of information into a small area. It might be the case that other methods, like graphs, are better for visualizing your results, yet you are often required to also include a table, so numerical values can be studied when so desired. For our example, we will use a nested regression with three models, which is a very common procedure in sciences. We will, therefore, run three different regression models, and save the results internally, so Stata can produce a combined output.

```
sysuse nlsw88, clear                                  //Load data
quietly regress wage c.ttl_exp                        //M1
estimates store M1
quietly regress wage c.ttl_exp i.union i.south        //M2
estimates store M2
quietly regress wage c.ttl_exp i.union i.south i.race //M3
estimates store M3
estimates table M1 M2 M3, se stats(r2 N)
```

https://doi.org/10.1515/9783110617160-010

Variable	M1	M2	M3
ttl_exp	.33142915	.32441171	.32679815
	.02540872	.01903674	.0189377
union			
union		1.060358	1.1783805
		.20604966	.20652253
south			
1		-1.2841683	-1.0257468
		.17909793	.18606967
race			
black			-.96975204
			.20640601
other			.55876262
			.77807283
_cons	3.6124924	3.6930569	3.7751123
	.3393469	.2740856	.27369685
r2	.07047787	.17309398	.18313975
N	2246	1878	1878

legend: b/se

The last line will tell Stata to produce a table which includes all three models, shows standard errors and also adds information about R-squared and the number of cases used. This looks quite fine, but still requires some more work. One problem is that the stars, which should indicate the p-levels, are missing. Also, it is a good idea to round numbers, say, to three decimal places.

Variable	M1	M2	M3
ttl_exp	0.331	0.324	0.327
	0.025	0.019	0.019
union			
union		1.060	1.178
		0.206	0.207
south			
1		-1.284	-1.026
		0.179	0.186
race			
black			-0.970
			0.206
other			0.559
			0.778
_cons	3.612	3.693	3.775
	0.339	0.274	0.274
r2	0.070	0.173	0.183
N	2246	1878	1878

legend: b/se

```
estimates table M1 M2 M3, se stats(r2 N) ///
    b(%7.3f) se(%7.3f)
```

This looks better. Getting this data into your text editor, for example Microsoft Word or LibreOffice Writer, can still be tricky. Highlight the table in Stata, right-click it and select "Copy Table". Then either go directly to your text editor, right-click and choose "Paste as..." and see which option works best. Sometimes it can be helpful to paste the data into calculation software first, like Excel or Calc, to get better formatting, and copy this table into the text editor. After you have done this, add the stars manually and adjust options for a pretty look. A finished table might look something like this[1] (Table 10.1):

Table 10.1: Exemplary regression result table.

	Model 1	Model 2	Model 3
Work Experience [Years]	0.33***	0.32***	0.33***
	(0.03)	(0.02)	(0.01)
Union-Member		1.06***	1.18***
		(0.21)	(0.207)
South		−1.28***	−1.03***
		(0.18)	(0.19)
Race			
White			Ref.
Black			−0.97***
			(0.21)
Other			0.56
			(0.78)
Const.	3.61***	3.69***	3.78***
	(0.34)	(0.27)	(0.27)
R^2	0.07	0.17	0.18
N	2246	1878	1876

Note: * $p<0.05$; ** $p<0.01$; *** $p<0.001$
Data Source: NLSW88, own calculations.

The problem is that when using Stata onboard functions, you will need to do some extra work to create these tables, just as we want them. An alternative is a user-written package that can do most steps automatically.

---

[1] Please note that for nested models, number of cases should usually be identical. This is explained on page 106.

```
ssc install estout, replace
```

Now we run each model again and store the results using the *eststo* command:

```
eststo M1: regress wage c.ttl_exp
eststo M2: regress wage c.ttl_exp i.union i.south
eststo M3: regress wage c.ttl_exp ///
    i.union i.south i.race
esttab M1 M2 M3 using "new_table.rtf"              //Output table
```

The last command produces the table, and saves it in rtf-fomat in the current working directory. It can be opened in any word processing editor. When you want, you can also export the following file types: txt, csv, html and tex. *Esttab* offers a great variety of options, so you can customize your tables as you like them, and then save the code in a do-file, so you can use it for future work. The following example shows how powerful the command can be:

```
esttab M1 M2 M3 using "new_table.rtf",nogaps ///
    nomtitles r2 star(# 0.10 * 0.05 ** 0.01 *** 0.001) ///
    b(3) se label replace
```

Nogaps makes the table more compact, *nomtitles* hides the model names, *r2* shows R-squared for each model, *star* modifies which significance levels should be indicated, *b(3)* sets the numbers, rounded to three decimal places, *se* shows standard errors instead of t-values, *label* shows variable labels and *replace* overwrites any existing table with the same name in your working directory. If you also want to hide reference categories, include *nobase*.

10.2 Graphs

Regression tables are important, but can be hard to interpret, especially, when there are interactions present in your models. Graphs are an excellent way of visualizing desired effects, so even people who are not immersed in the topic can understand them (never forget: when you want to influence policy, you have to be understandable by the public). Stata brings some great tools to create these graphs.

Let's start with the basics. Maybe you just want to show your regression coefficients with standard errors, or even better, confidence intervals. There exists a CCS that can do this for you. Try

```
ssc install coefplot, replace           //Install CCS
regress wage c.ttl_exp i.union i.south i.race
coefplot, xline(0)
```

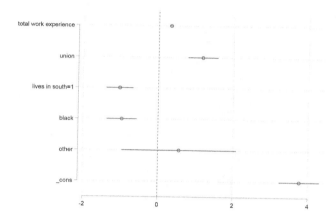

We use *coefplot* (Jann, 2014) to visualize the coefficients. The *xline* option adds a vertical bar. When the confidence interval of a variable crosses this line, we know that it is
not significant. As we see clearly, all variables have a significant effect (except "other"
in race, which is probably due to the low case number for this category 0.

This way we can visualize coefficients neatly. What if we want to predict wages
at special values, or for certain groups? No problem. But let's see how it works before
we get fancy. Just type

```
margins
```

```
Predictive margins                    Number of obs    =      1,878
Model VCE    : OLS

Expression   : Linear prediction, predict()
```

	Margin	Delta-method Std. Err.	t	P>|t|	[95% Conf. Interval]	
_cons	7.565423	.0870505	86.91	0.000	7.394697	7.73615

or click **Statistics → Postestimation → Marginal means and predictive margins**
and click **Submit**.

You will receive a single number (7.57). How can Stata summarize all variables used in
just one number? The estimated coefficients from the regression model above are used to
calculate the predicted wage for every person separately. Then Stata calculates the arithmetic mean of these predicted wages, which is our result. We can also calculate the marginal outcome at the mean, which (only in linear models) is identical to the current result:

```
margins, atmeans
```

```
Adjusted predictions                              Number of obs     =      1,878
Model VCE    : OLS

Expression   : Linear prediction, predict()
at           : ttl_exp          =     12.81837  (mean)
               0.union          =      .7545261 (mean)
               1.union          =      .2454739 (mean)
               0.south          =      .5745474 (mean)
               1.south          =      .4254526 (mean)
               1.race           =      .7204473 (mean)
               2.race           =      .2667732 (mean)
               3.race           =      .0127796 (mean)
```

	Margin	Delta-method Std. Err.	t	P>|t|	[95% Conf. Interval]
_cons	7.565423	.0870505	86.91	0.000	7.394697 7.73615

Stata also presents the empirical means found in the sample. You see that our "average" person has 12.8 years of job experience, and is 24.5% a union member. Calculating means for binary or ordinal variables is easy but a little nonsensical. Therefore, it is a good idea to move on and compute some better statistics, and not use the mean of all variables. Try

```
margins, at(ttl_exp=(0(5)30))
```

```
Predictive margins                                Number of obs     =      1,878
Model VCE    : OLS

Expression   : Linear prediction, predict()
1._at        : ttl_exp          =            0
2._at        : ttl_exp          =            5
3._at        : ttl_exp          =           10
4._at        : ttl_exp          =           15
5._at        : ttl_exp          =           20
6._at        : ttl_exp          =           25
7._at        : ttl_exp          =           30
```

	Margin	Delta-method Std. Err.	t	P>|t|	[95% Conf. Interval]
_at					
1	3.376404	.2578867	13.09	0.000	2.870629 3.88218
2	5.010395	.171756	29.17	0.000	4.673542 5.347248
3	6.644386	.1021103	65.07	0.000	6.444124 6.844648
4	8.278376	.0963573	85.91	0.000	8.089397 8.467355
5	9.912367	.1614768	61.39	0.000	9.595674 10.22906
6	11.54636	.2465697	46.83	0.000	11.06278 12.02994
7	13.18035	.3368238	39.13	0.000	12.51976 13.84094

Stata uses the last regression command to compute the wage of people at several numerical values of job experience, in our case from zero years up to 30 years, in steps of five years. Stata even produces a small table that tells you which values it uses, and then shows the results, including standard errors, in another table. This seems nice, but it gets even better by typing

```
marginsplot
```

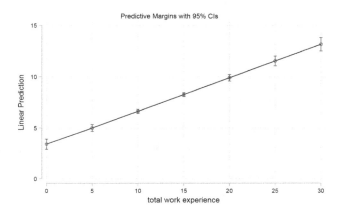

or click **Statistics** → **Postestimation** → **Margins plots and profile plots** and click **Submit**.

This is called a conditional-effects plot. What happens here is the following: Stata starts with the first number, which we specified in the command above (which is 0), and internally changes the experience of every single person to that value. Then it predicts, separately for each case, the wage, using the estimated regression coefficients with the individual information, except work experience, which was changed to zero. After that, it averages the predicted wages and reports them to repeat the process with the second specified value. This answers the question, what wages would be if every person had work experience of zero, with all other variables remaining unchanged.

We can do even better, when we differentiate not only by work experience but also by the status of union membership, so try

```
quietly margins union, at(ttl_exp=(0(5)30))
marginsplot
```

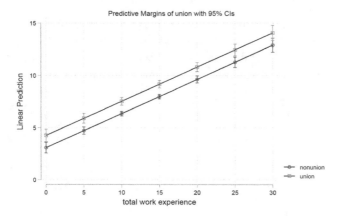

Here the list of computed values gets large so the *marginsplot* command is really a boon. We can clearly see that union members will always make more than non-members.

We can include as many variables as we want in the *at* option, for example, to differentiate by region. But this brings a lot of information into one graph, so instead we want subgraphs by union membership:

```
quietly margins union, at(ttl_exp=(0(5)30) south=(0 1))
marginsplot, by(south)
```

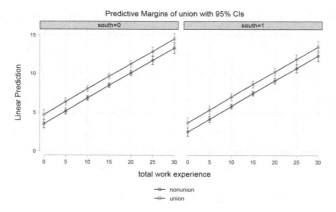

You can run the last command again (marginsplot), without any options, and decide which you prefer (one VS two graphs). The general interpretation is easy: union-members make more than others, but there are also differences for the regions, as people from the south seem to make less than other people.

Until now the graphs presented only consist of straight lines, as there are no interactions present (for an explanation see page 94). Let's change that by typing

```
regress wage c.ttl_exp##c.ttl_exp i.union i.south ///
    i.race
```

- output omitted -

For the sake of demonstration, we introduced an interaction between job experience and itself (higher ordered term), although usually these decisions should be theory-driven. We can obtain results by typing

```
quietly margins union, at(ttl_exp=(0(5)30) south=(0 1))
marginsplot, by(south)
```

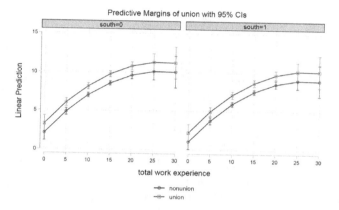

The lines are not straight anymore. Yet we can also learn from the regression output that, in general, the interaction does not make our model any better and we would not report this in a paper (see the p-values for the interaction-term).

You have learned that *margins* is a very powerful command, with a great number of options and possibilities that cannot be introduced here. To see more, refer to Williams (2012)[2] or have a look at the Stata help files for *margins* and *marginsplot*. On the website, you will find another do-file that contains more information about graphics and interaction effects.

---

2 A shorter presentation of it can be found at https://www3.nd.edu/~rwilliam/stats/Margins01. pdf (2018-01-26).

11 Writing a seminar paper

As you reach the end of this book, you are finally familiar with the basics of Stata. You are able to open and save Stata files, transform and create variables, compute descriptive statistics and work on more advanced methods like multiple regressions. This gives you all the tools to write solid research papers. If you use this book as a companion for your first paper ever written with Stata, the following guide should give you a very concise overview of how a seminar paper can be structured. This basic outline will be valid for every field of study, but make sure that you get additional input from your fellow students, colleagues or advisors.

11.1 The basic structure

1. Introduction: the beginning of your report should be dedicated to showing your motivation; why you care about your research topic and how it is relevant to the public. Use unsolved problems, or conflicting results, as a base and proceed to outline the basic structure of the paper, where you describe what you plan to do, which theories you will employ and which methods you will apply. Formulate a clear and concise research question that is manageable within the scope of your paper. Questions like "The causes of poverty" are usually a bad idea for a 15-page paper, as they could fill entire libraries. Finding and pinpointing the research question is a crucial step that might take some time, but will greatly affect the quality of your work. Also, briefly present the current state of research, and demonstrate the contribution of your research to the field.
2. Theoretical framework: in this section you introduce the theories you will use to guide your research. Whether you use a grand-theory, or more empirically driven approaches, depends on your field, research question and style. Make sure that you dig into the relevant literature, so you know the important aspects that are used by other researchers. Formulate hypotheses that you want to test empirically. Make sure that these are compact and testable ones (usually from one up to three, for a seminar paper). They should have the form of: "The higher the value of variable X, the lower the value of variable Y" (H1)." See page 83 for an example.
3. Your hypotheses should follow logically from the theories you have outlined before. Do not explain your theoretical foundations in their entirety, as only about 20% of your paper should be dedicated to this section. The intellectual challenge is to extract the theoretical parts and mechanisms that are relevant to your research question, from the main theories which might fill entire books.
4. Descriptive statistics: when you start with the empirical part, it is important to introduce your dataset: who created it, how it was obtained, and which methods were used. Introduce the operationalization, which is about the variables you

https://doi.org/10.1515/9783110617160-011

want to use, and how they are suited to your theories. It is relevant to explain how theoretical constructs, and actual variables, can be matched with each other and where deviations and problems lie. For example, when you need age of a pupil, as a control variable, because it is required by your theoretical framework, but only the class a pupil is in, is available, it is an important task to justify why it might be adequate to use this variable instead.

Then, write about the central variables you want to use, and report some basic information like means, standard deviations or distributions (using histograms, boxplots or kernel-density plots). You can use tables to display a lot of information in compact form. Remember that each causal question requires a good description, as this often enables you to understand the data and certain relationships within it. Furthermore, include some information about how your dependent and independent variable are related (use correlation coefficients or simple crosstabs). Briefly explain the methods you want to use, and why they are able to answer your research question.

5. Statistical analysis: here you proceed with your method, and report results, and also any problems that may arise. In the first part, you should just display these numbers without commenting on them. The second part, the discussion, is used to explain how your theoretical framework, statistical computations and results of other researchers fit together. When there are large deviations from your hypotheses, it is important to look for problems or reasons that could explain these differences (for example, those that may arise, due to different datasets, operationalization or methods).

6. Summary: shortly summarize your results, and try to answer the research question you formulated in the introduction, in a few sentences. Highlight certain aspects, results or problems that seem especially important. Furthermore, give an outlook on how you, or other researchers, should proceed in the future, after considering your results.

7. References: always include all references and citations used. It does not matter whether they are for theoretical argumentation, empirical research or about your methods. Remember, missing references can be viewed as plagiarism, so always double check that you have reported the origin of direct and indirect citations! Other researchers want to know your sources.

Note that this is a very general framework which can vary depending on your field, the extent of your research and the opinion of your advisor. It is always a very good idea to talk to him or her before you start writing, and present your ideas and plans, as you will receive some feedback that can help you enormously. Also, talk to fellow students, maybe from higher semesters, to learn about certain aspects or idiosyncrasies you should pay attention to. For example, whether you put your graphics and tables inside the chapters, or in a separate chapter at the end of the paper, is not written in stone. For a more detailed introduction refer to the paper of Bhakar and Nathani (2015).

11.2 Master do-files

In chapter two you have learned how you can use do-files to save commands and structure your tasks. When you work on larger projects, like a seminar paper, you will see that it is extremely helpful to have your files and data organized. Another trick you can use, is splitting different parts of analysis over several do-files. For example, you start with data recoding and operationalization, to transform your variables, so you can use them later. Then you proceed with descriptive statistics, which gives you an overview of the data. After that, you switch to statistical methods and run your regressions (or whatever methods you want to use). You can use a different do-file for each part, and later run them sequentially with a Master-Do. The first step is to create each file, say operationalization.do, descriptives.do and analyses.do. Then you create a new file, master.do, which you put in the same folder as the other ones. In this do-file you write

```
***Master do-file***
do operationalization
do descriptives
do analyses
```

When you run the Master-Do, all the other do-files will be called in the sequence that you placed them. By doing this, you can organize and automatize your workflow even better. When you do not want to see the actual output of a do-file, for example when data is recoded, use

```
quietly do operationalization
```

When you later come back and see that you forgot to create an important variable, edit your operationalization.do and run the Master-Do again. You can also combine this design with logs, so you will receive a complete output in a file after the do-files are finished.

12 The next steps

This final chapter will summarize information about where you can get help with Stata, and which sources are great for learning more and gaining further experience. As the program is quite popular, and beloved by many people, there are large communities, projects, websites, and forums that offer plenty of information and advice for beginners.

12.1 Online sources and manuals

- *Statalist.org* is the official Stata forum and usually offers the best advice when you have very special questions about Stata. Expert users and Stata employees will deal with your requests. When you use complex designs or methods and want to learn more about the details, this is the first place to go.
- *Reddit.com/r/Stata* is the Stata subforum on Reddit, and also highly popular. This seems like the perfect place for beginners who want to find typos in their commands, and need general help for questions that might have been asked before.
- *Talkstats.com* is mainly focused on general advice when it comes to statistics but also includes a Stata subforum.
- Stata Manual: every Stata installation comes with a tremendous documentation, which you can access either directly inside Stata (see page 23) or as PDFs which are saved on the computer. These manuals are sorted by topic, so you can browse freely and see which commands might be interesting for you.
- *Statabook.com*, the website of this book, also provides more material online, like do-files that contain additional information, and exemplary seminar papers that show, in-depth how the process of writing an empirical paper works.

12.2 Books

There are plenty of great books about Stata. I only want to introduce a few which might be interesting for the beginner.
- Kohler and Kreuter (2012): this is actually *the* book for the motivated beginner. The authors give a profound and in-depth presentation of how to use Stata, and furthermore, introduce the basic concepts of statistics. If you read the current book, as an absolute beginner, and want to get more information, this is clearly the next book you should pick up.
- Acock (2014): the structure of this book closely resembles the one of Kohler and Kreuter, and offers the interested beginner a more in-depth explanation of all tools and functions, starting with basic data management, and exploring more advanced methods. Whether you choose this one, or the one listed before, is up to you.

https://doi.org/10.1515/9783110617160-012

- Hamilton (2013): this book also offers an introduction to general themes like data management and visualizing, but mostly works as a grand-tour of the long list of methods Stata provides. Many kinds of regressions, survival analysis, event-history design and multilevel models are covered, as well as many more. While not offering a large theoretical introduction to each method, which would clearly go beyond its scope, the explanations are understandable, even for the beginner. This book is ideal in combination with an introductory course in methods, or just for browsing and exploring Stata's vast possibilities.
- Mehmetoglu and Jakobsen (2017): this quite recent work comes for students in a hurry, who have to work with advanced methods. While the introduction to the general Stata workflow is quite short, it offers applied knowledge and examples for basic regression models, and also more advanced techniques, like working with panel data. It is similar to the work of Hamilton, but much shorter and with a smaller scope.
- Long (2009): this is not a general introduction to Stata, but mostly deals with data management and organization. When you are not focused on direct application, but want to learn how you can structure your entire workflow around Stata, maybe for larger projects like a Ph.D. or your research career, then this book is for you.

References

Acock, Alan C. (2014): A Gentle Introduction to Stata. College Station, Texas.

Becker, Sascha O.; Caliendo, Marco (2007): Sensitivity analysis for average treatment effects, in: The Stata Journal 7(1): 71–83.

Best, Henning; Wolf, Christoph (2015): Linear Regression, in: Best, Henning; Wolf, Christoph (eds.): Regression Analysis and Causal Inference. London: 57–81.

Bhakar, Sher Singh; Nathani, Navita (2015): A Handbook on writing Research Paper in Social Sciences. Available online: https://www.researchgate.net/publication/282218102_A_Handbook_on_writing_Research_Paper_in_Social_Sciences (2018-07-23).

Bischof, Daniel (2017): New Graphic Schemes for Stata: plotplain & plottig, in: The Stata Journal 17(3): 748–59.

Caliendo, Marco; Kopeinig, Sabine (2008): Some Practical Guidance for the Implementation of Propensity Score Matching, in: Journal of Economic Surveys 22(1): 31–72. Available online: https://www.econstor.eu/bitstream/10419/18336/1/dp485.pdf (2018-02-02).

De Vaus, David (2001): Research Design in Social Research. London.

DiPrete, Thomas A.; Gangl, Markus (2004): Assessing bias in the estimation of causal effects: Rosenbaum bounds on matching estimators and instrumental variables estimation with imperfect instruments, in: Sociological methodology 34(1): 271–310.

Elwert, Felix (2013): Graphical Causal Models, in: Morgan, Stephen (Ed.): Handbook of Causal Analysis for Social Research. Dordrecht: 245–73. Available online: http://citeseerx.ist.psu.edu/viewdoc/download?doi=10.1.1.364.7505&rep=rep1&type=pdf (2018-07-07).

Elwert, Felix; Winship, Christopher (2014): Endogenous Selection Bias: The Problem of Conditioning on a Collider Variable, in: Annual Review of Sociology 40: 31–53. Available online: http://www.annualreviews.org/doi/abs/10.1146/annurev-soc-071913-043455 (2018-01-25).

Gebel, Michael (2009): Fixed-Term Contracts at Labour Market Entry in West Germany: Implications for Job Search and First Job Quality, in: European Sociological Review 25(6): 661–75.

Groves, Robert; Fowler, Floyd Jr.; Couper, Mick; Lepkowski, James; Singer, Eleanor; Tourangeau, Roger (2004): Survey Methodology. Hoboken.

Hamilton, Lawrence C. (2013): Statistics with Stata. Boston.

Hernán, Miguel A. (2018): The C-Word: Scientific Euphemisms Do Not Improve Causal Inference from Observational Data, in: AJPH 108(5): 616–19.

Hoekstra, Rink; Morey, Richard D.; Rouder, Jeffrey N.; Wagenmakers, Eric-Jan (2014): Robust misinterpretation of confidence intervals, in: Psychonomic Bulletin & Review 21(5): 1157–64.

Jann, Ben (2007): fre: Stata module to display one-way frequency table. Available from http://ideas.repec.org/c/boc/bocode/s456835.html (2018-01-18).

Jann, Ben (2014): Plotting regression coefficients and other estimates, in: The Stata Journal 14 (4): 708–37.

Jann, Ben (2017): kmatch: Stata module for multivariate-distance and propensity-score matching. Available online: https://ideas.repec.org/c/boc/bocode/s458346.html (2018-02-05).

King, Gary; O. Keohane, Robert; Verba, Sidney (1995): Designing Social Inquiry. Scientific Inference in Qualitative Research. Princeton.

King, Gary; Nielsen, Richard (2016): Why Propensity Scores Should Not Be Used for Matching (Working Paper). Available online: https://gking.harvard.edu/files/gking/files/psnot.pdf (2018-02-02).

King, Gary; Roberts, Margaret E. (2015): How robust standard errors expose methodological problems they do not fix, and what to do about it, in: Political Analysis 23(2): 159–79.

Kohler, Ulrich; Kreuter, Frauke (2012): Data Analysis using Stata. College Station, Texas.

Long, Scott (2009): The Workflow of Data Analysis Using Stata. College Station, Texas.

https://doi.org/10.1515/9783110617160-013

Long, Scott; Freese, Jeremy (2014): Regression Models for Categorical Dependent Variables Using Stata. College Station, Texas.

Matthews, Robert (2000): Storks Deliver Babies (p=0.008), in: Teaching Statistics 22(2): 36–38.

Mehmetoglu, Mehmet; Jakobsen, Tor Georg (2017): Applied Statistics Using Stata: A Guide for the Social Sciences. London.

Meuleman, Bart; Loosveldt, Geert; Emonds, Viktor (2015): Regression analysis: Assumptions and diagnostics, in: Best, Henning; Wolf, Christoph (eds.): Regression Analysis and Causal Inference. London: 83–110.

Mitchell, Michael N. (2012): A Visual Guide to Stata Graphics. College Station, Texas.

Mood, Carina (2010): Logistic Regression: Why We Cannot Do What We Think We Can Do, and What We Can Do About It, in: European Sociological Review 26(1): 67–82. Available online: http://www.urbanlab.org/articles/Mood_2010_LogRegession.pdf (2018-02-21).

Morgan, Stephen L.; Winship, Christopher (2015): Counterfactuals and Causal Inference: Methods and Principles for Social Research. Cambridge.

Pearl, Judea (2009): Causality: models, reasoning, and inference. Cambridge.

Pearl, Judea; Mackenzie, Dana (2018): The book of why. The new science of cause and effect. New York.

Rabe-Hesketh, Sophia; Skrondal, Anders (2012): Multilevel and Longitudinal Modeling Using Stata. Volume I: Continuous Responses. College Station, Texas.

Rosenbaum, Paul R. (2002): Observational Studies. New York.

Shadish, William; Cook, Thomas; Campbell, Donald (2002): Experimental and Quasi-Experimental Designs for Generalized Causal Inference. Boston.

Williams, Richard (2012): Using the margins command to estimate and interpret adjusted predictions and marginal effects, in: The Stata Journal 12(2): 308–31.

Wooldridge, Jeffrey M. (2016): Introductory econometrics: a modern approach. Boston.

Copyright

All tables and figures are, if not otherwise stated, created by the author. Figure 3.3 (page 26) was created based on a graphic originally uploaded by "Thirunavukkarasye-Raveendran" under the Attribution 4.0 International (CC BY 4.0) license, see:

https://commons.wikimedia.org/wiki/File:Zahlenstrahl_v1_02-11-2016_PD.svg

https://doi.org/10.1515/9783110617160-014

Index

https://doi.org/10.1515/9783110617160-015

Printed in the USA
CPSIA information can be obtained
at www.ICGtesting.com
JSHW062122310724
67371JS00008B/238

9 783110 617290